DURHAM

Where Visions Become Reality

Presented to:

DURHAM

Where Visions Become Reality

RIVERBEND BOOKS

A division of BOOKHOUSE GROUP, INC.

EDITOR Rob Levin

PUBLISHER Barry Levin

PROJECT MANAGER Cheryl Sadler

MARKETING MANAGER Rob Waller

PHOTO EDITOR Chuck Young

SENIOR WRITER Regina Roths

FINANCIAL MANAGER Julie Burton

JACKET AND BOOK DESIGN Jill Dible

PHOTOGRAPHERS
Bruce Feeley, Ken Hawkins, David Murray, Tim Wright, and Chuck Young

Riverbend Books wishes to thank the staff from the Greater Durham Chamber of Commerce for its assistance and guidance in publishing *Durham—Where Visions Become Reality*. Without its support, this book would not have been possible.

RIVERBEND BOOKS
A division of BOOKHOUSE GROUP, INC.

Published by Riverbend Books
an Imprint of Bookhouse Group, Inc.
818 Marietta Street
Atlanta, Georgia 30318
(404) 885-9515

ISBN: 1-883987-10-5

Chuck Young

David Murray

Table of Contents

CORMETECH

FOX50

RTI

MECHANICS AND FARMERS BANK
Come Home To More.

NORTH CAROLINA MUTUAL
LIFE INSURANCE COMPANY

Triangle
Orthopaedic
Associates, PA

**Stubbs, Cole, Breedlove,
Prentis & Biggs, P.L.L.C.**

Foreword

Durham, North Carolina—home of the world-renown Research Triangle Park, "Where the Minds of the World Meet." Home of prestigious Duke University and the 2001 NCAA Men's Basketball Champion Duke Blue Devils. Home of the American Dance Festival, dubbed by the *New York Times* as today's greatest dance ensemble. Home to the Durham Bulls, the AAA minor league franchise immortalized in the film classic "Bull Durham." And home of the North Carolina School of Science and Mathematics, the nation's first public residential high school for juniors and seniors demonstrating high aptitude for science and math.

Durham is a community with a genuine sense of place. Our unique character allows us to accommodate high-tech investment that harmonizes with our commitment to historic preservation. This progressive economic development process is on display in our central business district, where a tobacco company's former research space has been converted into a high-tech incubator that has spawned numerous biomedical and pharmaceutical start-up firms. So when you see twenty-first century research laboratories in the midst of nineteenth century tobacco factories and textile mills, you know you are in Durham, where those once vibrant industries gave way to the biotechnology and specialized health care that warrants our moniker: City of Medicine, USA.

The Research Triangle Park (RTP) is our pride and joy and has served as a magnet to attract the dynamic enterprises that have chosen to locate here. These firms thrive in Durham, fulfilling the goal of RTP's founders: to attract capital investment and create quality jobs by touting our higher educational institutions and the bright students they graduate. And with North Carolina Central University and Durham Technical Community College joining Duke, an exemplary town-gown partnership has been forged that yields palpable benefits to both academia and business. The corporate campuses emulate the tranquil setting of our local college campus-

es: high-level intellectual inquiry requires peace and solitude in order to be creative and productive.

But it is Durham's people that make this community special. We were selected by *FORTUNE Magazine* as the best place to work in America. *MONEY Magazine* named us the best place to live in the country. With a rich tradition of Southern hospitality, Durham has in many ways become a global village, an evolution that has occurred over many decades. The Duke family established and operated state-of-the-art manufacturing enterprises in the nineteenth century that led to the formation of the Duke Endowment and the University in the 1920s. The Spaulding, Merrick, and Moore families launched North Carolina Mutual Life Insurance Company in 1898, a harbinger of Mechanics and Farmers Bank and Mutual Community Savings and Loan that led to Durham's notoriety as the Black Wall Street of America. The Hill family established Central Carolina Bank, located in the heart of our downtown, and will celebrate its one hundredth anniversary in 2003—testimony to Durham's financial prowess and longevity.

So as you peruse these pages that display our community so vividly, we hope you will consider joining us. And if you already call Durham home, we thank you for making Durham so special. For as one of our leading citizens, Dr. LeRoy Walker, president emeritus of the United States Olympic Committee, declares: "What we have here is what others try to emulate."

Tom White
President & CEO
Greater Durham Chamber of Commerce

Chuck Young—All

The Bimbé Cultural Arts Festival has been a family affair in Durham for more than three decades. In reflection of the harvest festival of West Africa, for which the celebration is named, Bimbé is a feast of the collective talents of those artists influenced by West African traditions. For two days, the area's residents enjoy music, local and national entertainers, a market bazaar, folklore, and cultural foods. Youngsters can also find a world of unexplored wonders in the Kids Village.

Spring is a delightful time of year for families to get out-of-doors and enjoy family, gardening, and the first blooming of daffodils. Here mother Joanna Sawin delights her daughter, Julia, with the art of blowing bubbles.

Tim Wright—Both

Durham Marriott at the Civic Center

Whether staying in Durham for business or pleasure, one downtown hotel rises above the others in service and comfort—the Durham Marriott at the Civic Center invites guests to relax and enjoy a superior stay.

Upon entering the Durham Marriott, guests find themselves in a soaring atrium lobby, enhanced by stylish decor and flowing fountains. That welcome feeling is enhanced by a staff that wears hospitality like a badge of honor. The Marriott's management team represents decades of experience, backed by Marriott's commitment to service and excellence in every detail. "Of Course I Can" is the motto here, with every employee taking responsibility for guest satisfaction. Each employee at the Durham Marriott "owns" any question or concern that arises, taking care to resolve an issue personally whenever possible or finding the appropriate department to take charge

Below: The plaza's lush landscaping and flowing water-falls provide a calming, natural ambience for guests of this downtown hotel. As part of the Civic Center complex, Marriott guests can take care of business and partake of cultural activities while enjoying a comfortable stay. Right: Hotel guests can join "the locals" at The Bull Pen Sports Bar. This upscale sports bar reflects the hotel's close ties with the world famous Durham Bulls.

David Murray

Chuck Young

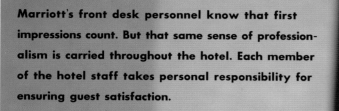

Marriott's front desk personnel know that first impressions count. But that same sense of professionalism is carried throughout the hotel. Each member of the hotel staff takes personal responsibility for ensuring guest satisfaction.

David Murray

Flexibility is the key to Marriott's ability to answer any catering need. While the plaza provides a beautiful setting for outdoor receptions, the adjacent Carolina Theatre offers an elegant, unique backdrop for gatherings.

of the matter. That in-house service philosophy combined with the application of Marriott's own "20 Basics," a list of simple hospitality axioms, makes every encounter between guest and staff a pleasant one.

Conveniently located in the heart of the city, the Marriott adjoins the Durham Civic Center, the premier meeting place for events of every variety and size. Managed and represented by the hotel, the Civic Center's Grand Ballroom, Exhibit Hall, and sectional meeting areas provide Durham with more than 40,000 square feet of convention space. In addition to complete catering services for the Civic Center, the hotel can arrange all audio-visual and presentation equipment.

Many hotel groups make use of the adjacent Carolina Theater, a beautifully restored theatrical venue that is accessible through the Marriott's prefunction space. The hotel and theater surround a relaxing fountain and tree-filled plaza area, creating an elegant setting for any gathering.

Local companies, corporations, and state and national association groups all enjoy the spacious, first-class accommodations at the Marriott. One hundred eighty seven guestrooms feature two phone lines, voice mail, dataports, and all the amenities to make any stay one of convenience and comfort. Guest rooms offer special features for the business traveler, and the concierge level provides upgraded service. Business travelers also have access to the hotel's twenty-four-hour business center, which includes copier, fax, and modem availability.

Following Marriott's traditionally high standards in food and beverage quality, The Bull City Steak House offers delicious buffet choices for both breakfast and lunch and its dinnertime menu features a tasty array of Prime Angus Beef, seafood, and pasta selections. For the individual traveler or for casual gatherings, lighter fare is available in The Bull Pen Sports Bar. Here guests and locals alike relax and enjoy a complete selection of beverages amid decor accentuated with memorabilia from The Bulls, Durham's legendary AAA baseball team.

Taking in a game at the nearby stadium is just one of the entertainment options available to Marriott guests. Other exciting places to explore include the Brightleaf Square restaurant and entertainment district, the Northgate and South Square malls, the Hayti Heritage Center, and the Museum of Life and Science. Registered guests are also invited to take advantage of the complimentary use of the state-of-the-art health club facilities at the adjacent Durham YMCA, with its indoor lap pool, whirlpool, gymnasium, cardiovascular equipment, free weights, and weight machines.

The Marriott offers complimentary self-parking as well as valet parking for overnight guests. Its location is within minutes of Duke University, Duke University Medical School and Hospital, Research Triangle Park, the University of North Carolina, and North Carolina Central University, and makes it a perfect place for visitors to these facilities.

In addition to its role as a central gathering place in Durham, the Marriott is also host to numerous civic and community events and actively involved in a sig-

nificant number of local activities. Complementing the hotel's sponsorship is a devoted staff who enjoy participation in a variety of organizations and associations. This spirit of involvement begins with General Manager Charlie Roberts, a community activist who gives of his time and talent. Says Roberts, "We believe that we have an opportunity to be more than just a venue for many of the activities associated with Durham's vitality and growth. We want the Marriott to take a leadership position in contributing to a renaissance of the downtown Durham destination."

Every event arranged by the Marriott catering department is as important to the staff as it is to the client. That philosophy of service ensures that every detail receives attention, regardless of meeting size or need.

David Murray

The Durham Civic Center provides the perfect space for annual gatherings of the Greater Durham Chamber of Commerce. As manager of this meeting space, the Marriott signature of quality is conveyed in every event.

David Murray

Two blocks from Duke University's East Campus is an area where mills once hummed with activity. Today, Old West Durham is a national historic district filled with an eclectic blend of unique shops. Whether window shopping, perusing the locally-owned stores, or just strolling along the avenue, Ninth Street offers plenty to tempt the eye and the palate. The friendly copper frog sculpture captures Isabel Kovacs' attention. The frog is a longtime rotating landmark of the Native Threads shop along Ninth Street, and is the creation of a South Carolina father and sons' team. In the Forest Hills' neighborhood Rick Roccesano (right) trains his dog "Bart" on the importance of balancing a tennis ball on the top of his head.

David Murray–Both

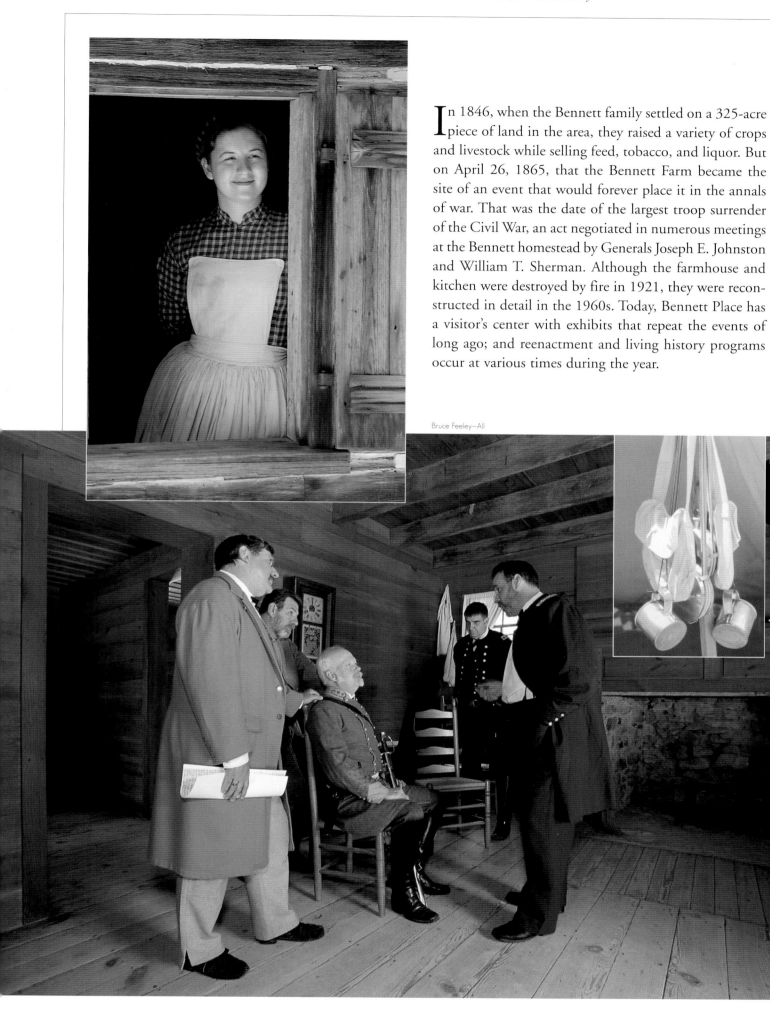

In 1846, when the Bennett family settled on a 325-acre piece of land in the area, they raised a variety of crops and livestock while selling feed, tobacco, and liquor. But on April 26, 1865, that the Bennett Farm became the site of an event that would forever place it in the annals of war. That was the date of the largest troop surrender of the Civil War, an act negotiated in numerous meetings at the Bennett homestead by Generals Joseph E. Johnston and William T. Sherman. Although the farmhouse and kitchen were destroyed by fire in 1921, they were reconstructed in detail in the 1960s. Today, Bennett Place has a visitor's center with exhibits that repeat the events of long ago; and reenactment and living history programs occur at various times during the year.

Bruce Feeley—All

Croasdaile Farm

After a day of life in the fast pace of the Triangle, many enjoy going home to the serenity of the country. For the residents of Croasdaile Farm, that sense of tranquility is only moments away.

Conveniently located on more than one-thousand acres of historic farmland in northern Durham, the Croasdaile Farm residential community blends elegant living with rural charm. While its close proximity to I-85 and the Durham Expressway gives Croasdaile Farm residents easy access to downtown Durham, Duke University, Research Triangle Park, and neighboring cities, a twenty year plan of development ensures that this community will never lose its pastoral beauty.

Single family homes make up the largest portion of Croasdaile Farm. Homesites amid rolling meadowlands and shady forests range in size from less than one acre to more than two acres. Buyers choose their own builders to create custom designs that meet established architectural standards which ensure the community's integrity is upheld. These standards also apply to the limited number of apartments and townhomes available within the community. Croasdaile Farm homes carry resale values ranging from $375,000 to over $2 million.

Spacious natural areas for all members of the family are an important part of Croasdaile Farm. Residents currently enjoy a forty acre woodland park and scenic

Ken Hawkins—Both

bodies of water, including the Dairy Pond and the six and one-half acre, fully stocked, Boles Lake, complete with fishing pier. Miles of walking paths make it easy for residents to enjoy the outdoors, and numerous gazebos offer places to gather or take a break in the shade.

Family is central to the Croasdaile Farm heritage. Forty years after John Sprunt Hill first farmed this extensive acreage in 1903, his daughter, Frances Hill

---

Left: The unique recreational pathway system in Croasdaile Farm is thoughtfully landscaped with informal plantings to complement the country atmosphere. Above: A singular residential opportunity, Croasdaile Farm is the perfect setting for the homes people have always wanted. Its rural heritage is the foundation for a unique community designed for people who share a simple appreciation for the understated beauty of natural surroundings.

Fox, and her husband Herbert, took over operations. By that time, the farm encompassed two dairies and was a well-known producer of tobacco, chickens, pigs and milk. In 1964, the couple began developing a part of the farm as Croasdaile, a distinguished residential community that now encompasses 200 exclusive homes, Croasdaile Country Club with its member-owned championship golf course, business and medical offices and a shopping center. Today, the adjacent Croasdaile Farm is being developed by third and fourth generations, George and David Beischer.

A half dozen Black Angus cattle still roam this graceful countryside, and in the future, the farm's existing silos and barns are planned to be converted to a village center with restaurant, retail and office space. But regardless of what develops at Croasdaile Farm, it will always be a peaceful refuge from the fast pace of life in this dynamic region.

Bruce Feeley—All

What began in 1976 as a group of musicians volunteering their time to offer free orchestral performances has grown to be the Durham Symphony Orchestra, a not-for-profit organization fostering music appreciation for the people of the Triangle. Led by Musical Director and Conductor Alan E. Neilson, the symphony's season includes classical concerts, guest artists, an outdoor family pops performance, and a holiday pops. The symphony encourages interest among youth through a young artists concert and other performances. The Durham Symphony also offers Rent-a-Symphony for special events of supporters.

Perhaps one of the most unique versions of a timeless literary work is that of The Vo-Du Macbeth. Set in New Orleans in 1865, the dramatic script, which is still under development, was performed by local actors from around the region at the Hayti Heritage Center in the spring of 2001. The reading, presented through a collaboration between St. Joseph's Historic Foundation and the National Spirit Project, was accompanied by a discussion of other issues in African-American culture and history.

Ken Hawkins—All

Syngenta Biotechnology, Inc.

In the past thirty years, farmers around the world have increased food production dramatically—largely through the use of improved fertilizers, higher-yielding seeds and effective weed and pest control products. But will agriculture be able to keep up with the growing demand for more and better food in the next thirty years?

Scientists at Syngenta Biotechnology, Inc. (SBI), in Research Triangle Park, N.C., are doing their part to support farmers by using a combination of centuries-old scientific theory and cutting-edge modern technology

Syngenta Biotechnology, Inc., is one of four global research facilities for Syngenta, a world-leading agribusiness. Based in Basel, Switzerland, Syngenta has more than twenty thousand employees around the world, helping farmers grow better crops by providing high-quality seeds and improved solutions for weed, disease and pest control.

to develop the crop production products of tomorrow.

The roots of SBI run deep in the Research Triangle Park community. Ciba-Geigy (a company which is now part of Syngenta) first established a biotechnology research facility here in 1983. The facility has grown and developed, including expansion of the labs and greenhouses in 2000. Today, more than 270 scientists and support personnel work at the SBI facility, and are imbedded in the fabric of RTP's civic and non-profit groups and schools.

SBI researchers come from some of the most prestigious agricultural universities in the world, and bring a breadth of experience in plant genetics, molecular biology, cell biology, chemistry and biochemistry. They are combining very different techniques from genetic enhancement of plants to "high throughput screening" which allows efficient evaluation of the potential value of thousands of chemical or biological compounds. Their common

Chuck Young—All

An SBI scientist examines corn plants in greenhouse breeding trials. Greenhouse studies are a critical step in turning scientific discoveries found in the laboratory into productive and profitable products for farmers to use in their fields.

ambition is using science to unlock the secrets of nature for the development of practical, commercial solutions to challenges facing farmers, consumers and our environment.

A few areas of focus include:

Preventing crop loss to plant diseases. Agricultural crops are exposed to thousands of fungi and other disease organisms that can literally rot crops in the field. Research at SBI is exploring better in-field diagnostic tests for crop diseases to help farmers find and treat problems earlier. Research is also exploring ways to increase the activity of a plant's own disease defense systems—a sort of natural "vaccination." Finally, SBI scientists are exploring ways to insert new genes into specific crops to impart immunity to key plant diseases.

Preventing insect feeding damage. One of the early successes of biotechnology has been the ability to insert genes from a naturally occurring Bacillus thuringiensis (Bt) bacterium into corn, cotton and other crops to impart internal protection from insect feeding. For many farmers, Bt crops are a more productive and profitable option. These crops are proving to be a valuable tool for popular "integrated crop management" programs and are thus making new pest control choices possible for farmers.

Improving weed control programs. For decades, farmers have used a combination of tillage and chemical herbicides to control yield-robbing weeds in crops. Advances in biotechnology have made weed control more efficient and cost-effective in soybeans and other crops by producing crops that are resistant to broad-spectrum herbicides that would otherwise damage the crop.

Improving food quality. Another objective of ag biotechnology research is improving the quality and nutritional benefits of food crops. While this research is still in its infancy, early promise is seen from grains with improved vitamin content or vegetables with increased levels of dietary antioxidants that may reduce cancer and other human diseases.

The needs of our growing global population will continue to put pressure on agriculture in coming decades. Scientists at Syngenta Biotechnology, Inc., hope their efforts will provide valuable new tools for farmers to rise to the challenge.

Top: An SBI scientist inspects dishes containing transgenic seedlings. One modern biotechnology technique is to identify a specific gene that creates a desired characteristic or trait and then insert that DNA into plant cells. At this point, the enhanced cells are "transformed" and grown into plants that can be used to produce the seeds farmers use to grow improved crops. Above: SBI scientists load samples into a DNA analyzer, then read the computer-generated chromatogram of the analysis. DNA is the basic genetic blueprint of a cell, and analyzing and understanding the DNA structure is the first step in helping scientists develop plants with specific, desirable characteristics.

After a $1.5 million renovation that closed the facility for four years, Hillside Park pool reopened in 2000. The project included a new pool with sprayground, bathhouse, concession stand, an amphitheater, a picnic shelter, and a multipurpose court. A new sidewalk also connects the park to the W.D. Hill Recreation Center. The renovation completely revitalized a park that had fallen into disarray once the pool closed because of plumbing and other problems. The "sprayground" is irresistible to Micheala Burton, while Teri Johnson and daughter Shayla (above right) enjoy the new playground at Hillside Park.

There are five high schools in the Durham Public School system, each dedicated to preparing students for work or education beyond graduation. Preparing students physically is part of that commitment and each year student athletes are challenged to be the best at the Quad Track and Field Championships. Held at Riverside High School, the meet brings teams from around the region to compete in running, jumping, relay, and other events.

Bruce Feeley—All

In 2001, North Carolina Central University (NCCU) hosted the Central Intercollegiate Athletic Association (CIAA) Outdoor Track and Field Championships. Although rival St. Augustine retained its men's and women's team titles, NCCU's Eagles held their own against the competition. Multi-champion Jason Smoots received the Most Outstanding Track Athlete crown for his winning times in both the 100- and 200-meter dashes. The CIAA athletic conference, established in 1912, is comprised of twelve higher learning institutions whose enrollments have historically been primarily African-American students. Five NCCU student athletes received recognition in 2001 by the CIAA for excelling in the classroom and on the field. Chosen as members of the CIAA Commissioner's All-Academic Team were Katerina Glosova, Lisa Hicks, Constance Murdock, Rachelle Zastoupil, and Lanelle Turner.

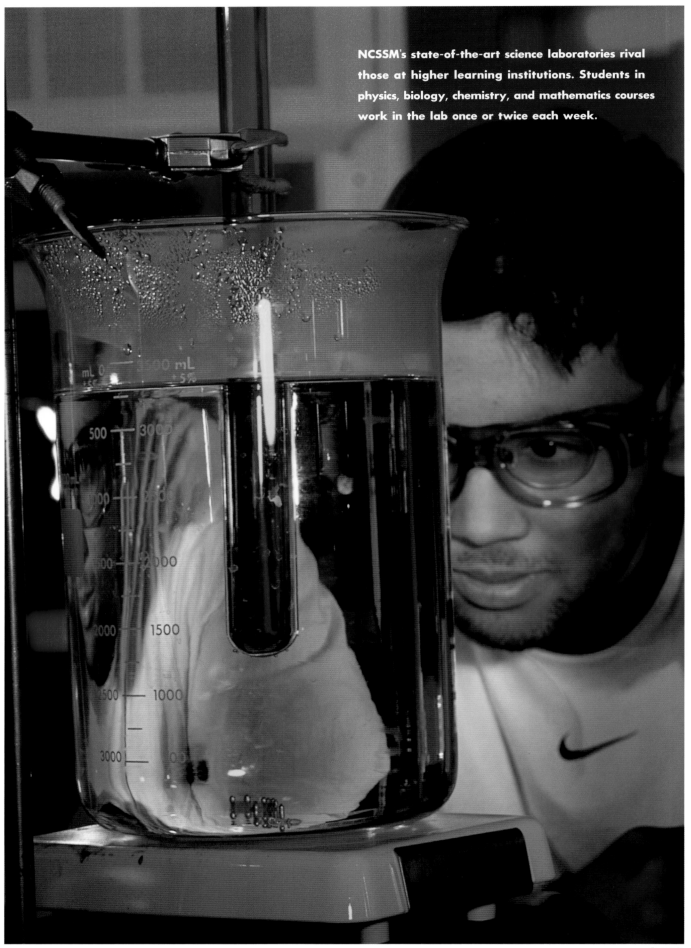

NCSSM's state-of-the-art science laboratories rival those at higher learning institutions. Students in physics, biology, chemistry, and mathematics courses work in the lab once or twice each week.

Tim Wright

The North Carolina School of Science and Mathematics

When The North Carolina School of Science and Mathematics (NCSSM) opened in 1980, its mission was twofold: to provide opportunity for residential students who possessed special talents in science and mathematics and to serve as a catalyst for improvement in these studies for students through grade twelve.

Today NCSSM has gained worldwide recognition and has grown to be a model for other science and math educational facilities.

Like all public high schools, entrance to NCSSM is not based on economic background. Instead, admission relies on a student's demonstrated interest and talent in science and mathematics combined with a blend of test scores, teacher recommendations, and on-campus interviews.

On a campus full of the best and brightest, NCSSM students bond through a shared interest in learning, building friendships that last a lifetime. Beyond science and mathematics, students have access to a full range of humanities studies including art, drama, and music. Extracurricular activities on campus range from tutorials and lectures to sports and student life programs.

Students of NCSSM also learn to be leaders. Outside the classroom, students participate in programs that teach valuable hands-on experience and time management skills. These programs include on-campus Work Service; hometown involvement through Community Service; and career exposure with the Mentorship Program.

Durham's diverse research, business, and cultural climate provides students with off-campus opportunities that entice many to remain in the area upon graduation. Nearly three-fourths of NCSSM graduates attend the state's colleges and a large majority become North Carolina teachers, researchers, medical professionals, and leaders of new and existing local businesses.

The NCSSM campus is quickly becoming a place for the community as well. Festivals such as the annual Native American Powwow bring thousands to the campus while student groups organize other ethnic and business activities. The recent completion of the $10 million John Friedrick Educational Technology Complex (ETC) now provides space for campus and community events such as performances, lectures, social gatherings, and student activities.

Gifts to the NCSSM Foundation continue to make updates in technology, renovation of campus historical buildings, and new structures such as the ETC possible. Through partnerships with both public and private interests, NCSSM has established its Education Future Center. The center is home to Cyber Central, which serves as the hub for NCSSM's Cyber Campuses, a seven classroom, technology-rich network that extends campus resources to sixty of the state's 100 counties. This outreach program is just one of the many ways NCSSM will continue to uphold its mission to improve the state's math and science opportunities.

Each spring, students take an eight-day break from regular classes to participate in specialized faculty-arranged mini-courses or student-designed academic projects. In 2001, three students explored the effects of patterns and voice on newly hatched chicks in an imprinting project.

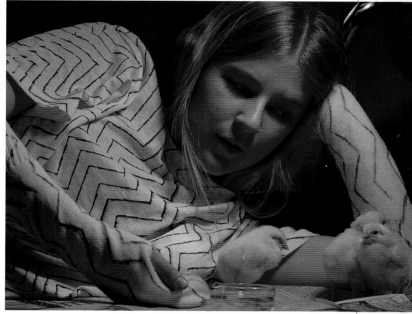

Bruce Feeley

Just north of Durham runs the Eno River, once the site of early settlers and nearly three dozen mills. Primary of these grist mills was the West Point Mill, focal point of a community that once contained a blacksmith shop, general store, saw mill, and cotton gin. Constructed in 1778, the mill was destroyed by a dam break in 1942 and reconstructed some thirty years later. Today, West Point Mill is a part of the historic West Point on the Eno city park. Its wheels are once again turning through the aid of water and grinding grain into flour that is sold in the on-site store.

Nothing short of the finest in North Carolina cooking awaits at Bullock's Bar-B-Que. Sliced or chopped pork is the staple here. Add a side of slaw and some of Bullock's renowned hush puppies and you're eating the same favorites of the many celebs mounted on the "Wall of Fame." Bullock's is also known for its fried chicken, oysters, and a host of other calorie-laden, but oh-so-delicious items. The lines form early but move quickly at both lunch and dinner in this family-style restaurant on Quebec Drive.

Chuck Young–Both

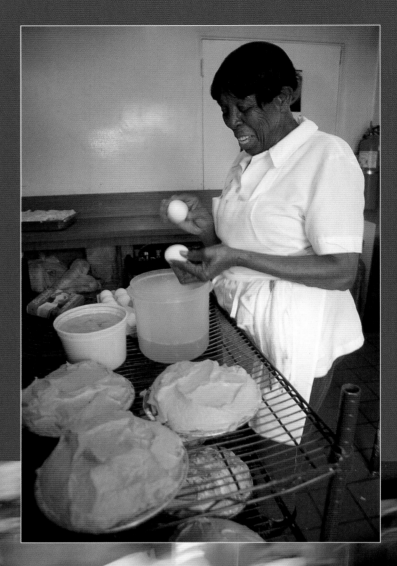

Durham—Where Visions Become Reality

Verizon

As a global telecommunications leader, Verizon offers comprehensive solutions for residential, business, and government customers. But while its telecommunications infrastructure is second-to-none, it is people that power this multinational corporation.

In order to understand the challenges affecting medium to large businesses in Durham and Research Triangle Park, Verizon account teams step out of the office and into the workplace of virtually every industry in the area. As representatives for a full line of manufacturers, these teams provide unbiased answers that range from voice to video to data. Verizon is also one of the world's largest providers of telephone directories and its extensive organization of support personnel work around the clock to ensure outstanding customer service.

Verizon's answers to business needs include participating in education and workforce training initiatives. Grants from the Verizon Foundation and the company's work with Durham Public Schools, the Durham Public Education Network, the Durham County Literacy Council, North Carolina

Central University, and Duke University are helping improve literacy. And with the Greater Durham Chamber of Commerce and the Durham Workforce Partnership, Verizon is making education relevant to the workplace through innovative school-to-work programs.

In order to bridge the digital divide, Verizon partnered with the marketing firm EasyWeb Inc. and others to develop computer learning centers complete with Internet access in Durham's public housing communities. Today, these resources are providing low-income children and adults with education, information, job prospects, and a world of opportunity.

(l-r) Erroll Reese, president of EasyWeb, Inc.; Carl Niemeyer, Manager-Verizon Solutions Center; and Steve Toler, regional director-public affairs for Verizon; in a videoconference from the high-tech telecommunications demo center. Reese, nationally recognized for his efforts to bridge the digital divide, is sharing his expertise with a Dallas party interested in the success of the Durham Community Learning Centers program.

Chuck Young

Perhaps nowhere is there a more perfect picture of rural North Carolina than at Quail Roost Farm. Built in the 1930s, this seven-hundred-acre working horse farm is one of the nation's top dairy and stable farms. Its nostalgic silos and four horse barns are surrounded by thousands of acres of countryside, rolling hills, woody stands, and a small pond. In addition to horse boarding and riding lessons, Quail Roost is the site of foxhunts of the Red Mountain Hounds hunt club.

David Murray

As one of the first autonomous African-American churches in the nation, St. Joseph's AME Church has served the Durham community for more than a century. Now a National Historic Landmark, the 1891 structure is a blend of Gothic Revival and Richardsonian Romanesque architecture. Among its twenty-three stained glass windows are tributes to past patrons Washington Duke, W.T. Blackwell, and Julian Carr. Today, the St. Joseph's Historic Foundation is working to renovate the sanctuary into a 300-plus seat performing arts center adjacent to the Hayti Heritage Center. (l-r) Senior Planner Steve Crews of the Durham City/County Planning Department and V. Dianne Pledger, president and CEO of St. Joseph's Historic Foundation (bottom) at the Hayti Heritage Center, review plans for the restoration. Once one of the South's largest estates, Historic Stagville is now dedicated to the preservation and study of African-American life and culture on the plantation. An original slave quarters and barn remain intact on the premises, revealing insight into a new culture that was formed from societies combined after their arrival in America. Sarah LeCovat and seven-month-old son Will (right) join others in learning about the self-reliant slave community that inhabited Stagville.

David Murray

Bruce Feeley

37

Greater Durham Chamber of Commerce

The character of Durham, North Carolina is a unique and charming blend of ethnic, global, and economic diversity. These exceptional qualities are born of a tobacco and textile heritage that has successfully transformed into technology, research, medicine, and industry. And fostering this bustling metamorphosis is the Greater Durham Chamber of Commerce, a group of more than 1,400 industries, businesses, and professional firms, that voluntarily participate in building a healthy economy and improved quality of life.

Like Durham, the Chamber is a multi-faceted entity, supporting programs that focus on economic development, government affairs, business assistance, and community promotion. Commitment to excellence in these areas of the community has helped

Durham rise in best cities rankings in both Fortune and Money magazines. The city has also ranked second nationally in international investment by Site Selection magazine and Durham County itself has been recognized as the strongest economically by Outlook North Carolina magazine.

Top recognitions like these stem in part from activities in Durham's thriving knowledge-based, high-technology industries that range from bio-pharmaceutical to electronics. As an economic development agency, the Chamber's involvement have helped create thousands of new jobs in these areas of industry, while generating millions in investments.

Continued growth in these sectors, combined with an outstanding level of technology transfer from both Duke and North Carolina Central universities, is only strengthening Durham's role as a leader in world-class "town-gown" partnerships.

The Chamber is actively involved in addressing business workforce needs while helping economically disadvantaged individuals participate in the area's thriving economy. Its Work First Job Developer, in collaboration with the Durham County Department of Social Services, has successfully placed hundreds of welfare recipients in good jobs. The program serves as a national welfare-to-work model.

With a rich tradition of African American business leadership that made Durham known as the nation's "Black Wall Street," Durham now holds the distinctive title of "The City of Medicine, U.S.A." The Chamber coordinates communication and activities that bring together mutual interests for both business and medicine. And while the manufacturing sector has undergone drastic change it is once again seeing substantial growth. The Chamber's efforts were instrumental in recruiting the largest industrial investment in the community's history securing Durham's future in automotive components manufacturing. Chamber support of cultural, educational, and civic endeavors continues to help Durham be an attractive location for multinational corporations from around the globe.

No doubt Chamber actions have generated results but its future goals are no less ambitious. These days the Chamber is actively involved in preserving and adaptively reusing the city's rich architectural heritage by attracting investment to the central core while maintaining the momentum that exists in suburban markets. Taken as a whole one thing is certain, the Greater Durham Chamber of Commerce will continue to build upon the diversity that makes this community an exciting place to be.

Ken Hawkins

One of the benefits of Chamber membership is the ability to network with other members and develop new business contacts, acquaintances, and opportunities. The Chamber offers these kinds of opportunities through activities such as Business After Hours, which is an informal reception held at different venues throughout the community.

Chuck Young—Both

David Murray

A mid the peaceful North Carolina landscape, golfers can enjoy an afternoon of eighteen holes on numerous public courses. Hillandale (left) has been a favorite public course for the golfers in and around Durham since 1913. Its Hillandale Golf Shop has received numerous accolades as one of the nation's top shops for golf products at reasonable prices. In 2001, Duke University Golf Club was the proud host of the NCAA Men's Championships. In an incredible display of college golf at its finest, the Florida Gators chomped the competition with a score of thirty-four under par in its last fifty-four holes of golf. Nick Gilliam (opposite top), from Florida State, took home the individual overall with a four-day score of twelve under at 276.

Chuck Young

WTVD ABC 11 Eyewitness News

Since 1954, WTVD has been broadcasting to viewers in the Raleigh-Durham-Fayetteville market. Today the station has become the Heart of Carolina's prime-time choice for popular programming on the ABC television network.

Local news is ABC 11's primary focus. "Viewers need to be informed and we take that responsibility very seriously," says Bruce Gordon, the station's president and general manager. The station's fast-paced newscast allows viewers to see stories for themselves through the experiences of eyewitnesses

ABC 11 Eyewitness News Anchors Larry Stogner and Miriam Thomas are two of the most recognized news personalities in the Heart of Carolina.

to news and events. Led by ABC 11 Eyewitness News anchors Larry Stogner, Miriam Thomas, Steve Daniels, Frances Scott, John Clark, Barbara Gibbs, and Scott Light, the station delivers award-winning news and information to television viewers throughout the Heart of Carolina.

Utilizing the latest in state-of-the-art technology, ABC 11 Eyewitness News takes pride in bringing live, up-to-the-minute news and information into viewer's homes. The station utilizes cutting-edge digital technology to broadcast breaking news from its Live Mobile Newsrooms stationed throughout the market. And ABC 11 Eyewitness News is the only station that provides live helicopter traffic reports during morning and evening rush hour periods.

Ken Hawkins

Tim Wright

ABC 11's commitment to local news and information is matched only by its commitment to strong community service programs. "We're citizens of this community and we think it's important to help all the people of Durham realize their dreams," says Gordon.

For the last fifteen years, ABC 11 has been the leader in the market in collecting food and cash donations for specific charitable causes. Since 1997, ABC 11's "Heart of Carolina Food Drive" has collected nearly a million pounds of food, and raised more than $670,000 to support The Food Bank of North Carolina.

In addition to substantial planned annual community service commitments, ABC 11 and the Eyewitness News team spring into action to support communities with vital news and information and needed financial relief whenever needs arise. When Hurricane Fran stormed directly through the Heart of Carolina in 1996, WTVD immediately began broadcasting vital information around the clock via television and radio. Through the supplemental sale of a commemorative videotape, the station raised an additional $100,000 for the Red Cross. ABC 11 also responded to 1999's Hurricane Floyd crisis with non-stop, commercial-free coverage for twenty-two and one-half hours . . . the only station to provide news and information at that level. Furthermore, the station immediately teamed with Kroger grocery stores, its food-drive partner, and raised 1.8 million pounds of food for the thousands of flood victims waiting a week for the storm's ten feet of water to recede.

Backed by the strength of its parent company ABC, and in turn The Walt Disney Company, WTVD and ABC 11 Eyewitness News will continue to unify viewers in the Heart of Carolina with information and news about the events that affect their lives.

SOCIETY

Leon Jordan's Continentals
Leon Jordan's Continentals
Leon Jordan's Continentals

Tim Wright–All

Twice a month, the Durham Armory really swings. That's because it's the perfect location for swing dancing to live music courtesy of the Triangle Swing Dance Society. On the first and third Saturdays of the month, hundreds come from miles around for some good old-fashioned fun in a smoke- and alcohol-free gathering. It doesn't matter if you know the steps, each dance begins with a free beginner's lesson. The group also holds workshops, socials, and other special events. Debra Ramsey and Wesley Boz (upper right) have a swinging time at the Armory.

RTI

One of the world's most valuable resources for turning knowledge into practice is the centerpiece of Research Triangle Park. This resource—Research Triangle Institute (RTI)—is an independent R&D organization dedicated to improving the human condition.

By its very nature, RTI nourishes innovation. Its worldwide staff of more than 1900 includes researchers from 115 disciplines who form project teams to tackle complex national and global problems. For example statisticians, chemists, engineers, and child development experts create new approaches for assessing children's exposure to pollutants. In addition, an interdisciplinary team of psychologists, ethnographers, and statisticians develop innovative strategies for curbing the global spread of HIV.

Besides health and medicine, RTI conducts innovative, multidisciplinary R&D in environmental protection, education and training, decision support and technology commercialization for clients in government, industry, and public service. Founded in 1958 by North Carolina's universities, RTI is quickly becoming recognized as the world's premier independent research organization.

To fulfill its mission of improving the human condition, RTI emphasizes getting the results of its research into the marketplace. Marketplace success also generates cash for more R&D, creating more discoveries to improve the lives of people around the world. In addition to licensing, RTI launches new companies and codevelops products with industry.

For example, RTI spin-off Ziptronix, Inc., commercializes technology for three-dimensional circuitry.

The campus-like setting for RTI's laboratories and offices encourages teamwork that crosses the boundaries of scientific disciplines. Shown here is the Gertrude M. Cox Statistics Building. RTI has multiple locations on four continents.

Ken Hawkins—All

RTI also has a business unit, RTI Health Solutions, to meet the product valuation needs of the pharmaceutical, biotechnology, and medical device industries. Among RTI's codevelopment projects is a partnership with a start-up company to commercialize pharmaceuticals for treating cocaine addiction.

RTI also makes its Virtual Emergency Medical Simulator available to civilian medical personnel. Like many RTI innovations, this virtual-reality application originated from government-funded R&D, in this case for training military medics. Another outgrowth of this R&D is a partnership with California's community colleges to address the shortage of nurses by creating on-line curricula.

RTI has an international reputation for excellence in transferring technology from government to industry, and from company to company. Recent developments for NASA include more than fifty licensing agreements to make the agency's intellectual property available for non-aerospace use. RTI helps its industry clients earn revenue by out-licensing technology to non-competing industries.

Other clients, ranging from the Department of Education to commercial media giants, turn to RTI for solutions to their survey research needs. RTI is a recognized leader in challenging, large-scale survey research and the innovative methods and technology such studies require.

RTI's collaborations naturally involve local universities. In addition to a variety of medical R&D collaborations with Duke University, RTI teams with the University of North Carolina at Chapel Hill to assess medical procedures, and with North Carolina State University on environmental R&D.

RTI's influence extends worldwide. Its work to change government policy and improve public institutions has brought public education to millions of children in Africa, increased access to health care in Southeast Asia, established sound environmental management by local governments in Central Europe, and enabled cities in former Soviet states to finance urban services such as transportation. RTI's work with governments, donor agencies, and industry facilitates global commercialization of new treatments for diseases such as tuberculosis, which infects two-thirds of the world's population.

Top: As a leader in Virtual Reality applications, RTI emphasizes technology-assisted learning in fields such as medicine, manufacturing, and maintenance. Here, VR director Sam Field tests a simulator that helps fleet operators train and evaluate drivers. Above: RTI brings fun and fitness to the workplace through a variety of recreation programs. Here, Lindsay James (front, center), an environmental economist and accomplished dancer, leads a Friday afternoon ballroom dancing class.

Famous for discovering the cancer drugs Taxol® and Camptothecin™, RTI scientists are creating pharmaceuticals for disorders such as addiction and pain. Here, chemist Nam-Cheol Kim analyzes herbal remedies to provide consumer information about efficacy and side effects.

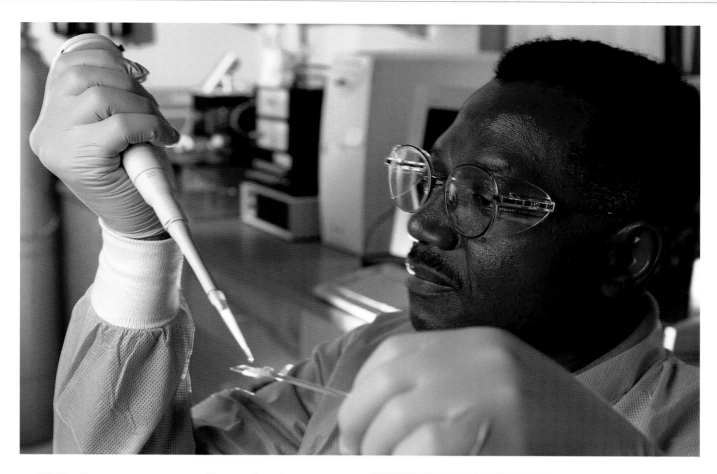

RTI's disease prevention efforts often begin with outreach programs in its home community. RTI secures grants for start-of-the-art public health programs, evaluates the results, and shares lessons learned with the social services community nationwide. RTI's community-based efforts in Durham and other North Carolina locales help reduce smoking prevalence, prevent youth violence, and prevent complications of diabetes among African-Americans.

For its accomplishments, RTI receives frequent recognition. Among its honors are the world's two most prestigious awards for pharmaceutical R&D, the Charles F. Kettering Prize for cancer research and the Alfred Burger Award for medicinal chemistry. RTI also has been recognized by NASA, EPA, and DOD for public service. Its staff members regularly receive top awards from professional societies, such as the American Public Health Association, the American Chemical Society, and the American Otologic Society.

With each of its innovative initiatives, RTI's focus remains fixed on better quality of life for people around the world. That focus makes RTI the world's best source for turning knowledge into practice

Top: Environmental laboratories at RTI emphasize accurate measurements of pollutants, understanding human and ecological impacts, and use technology to reduce emissions. Here, chemist Melville Richards tests a method to analyze tiny particles that may cause respiratory problems. Above: Reaching out to the local community through federally-funded public health initiatives, RTI improves the state of the art by evaluating the programs' effectiveness. Here, health educator Jaki Brown works on a woman-focused intervention to prevent HIV transmission.

through innovative, multi-disciplinary research and technology development.

One Durham business has literally kept its doors open by keeping a careful eye on the changing landscape of Durham. That business is Stone Bros. & Byrd, originally founded in 1914 as a farm supply store, now operating as a favorite lawn and garden center. One reason for the popularity of the downtown store is Managing Partner George Davis Jr.'s innovative ideas in lawn care. Some years back, Davis worked in conjunction with Lofts Seed Co. and NC State Univerity to create four lawn seed blends specifically for the area. "With four unique blends we can cover just about every situation around here," he says. "The blends depend on different degrees of sun and shade tolerance, but they're all adapted for Piedmont." Davis and his staff still sell seeds and a variety of other items the old-fashioned way by weighing and pre-bagging them in the store.

Whether it's crafting, movies, or reading programs, there's always something fun happening at the Durham County Library. Treston Breeden and Lauryn Vickers (below) are enthralled with the readings by Deborah Rogers Amos (left), and activities during storytime for the younger kids. Since 1897, the Durham County Library System has brought a world of learning to children of all ages. Today, 25 percent of its more than 450,000 books are children's reading. In addition to the main library and seven branches, the library brings books and materials to the community through its Bookmobile, its Older Adult and Shut-In Service (OASIS), and its Raise-A-Reader workshops for parents and childcare providers.

David Murray—Both

The Housing Authority of the City of Durham

There is a spirit of renewal in the city of Durham, fostered in part by the efforts of the Housing Authority of the City of Durham (DHA). The Durham Housing Authority is an organization that, along with providing shelter, affords many residents the foundation for a new beginning.

The primary role of the Durham Housing Authority is to provide its citizens with a place to call home. An equally important service is to bring together housing and program support in a way that helps people better help themselves. "We really want to break the cycle of dependency," says Executive Director James R. Tabron. "Our goal is to assist individuals and families in reaching higher levels of personal and economic self sufficiency." No agency can do this alone and DHA works hand in hand with a host of service providers in Durham.

DHA helps residents succeed through programs that assist them in all areas of life. "We want to complement the efforts of those persons who move into our housing so that they can move up and move out," says Tabron. DHA encourages education through programs such as the Student Attendance Incentive and the Ruffin/Edwards Academic Development Scholarship programs. Clients can also benefit from career development workshops and business ventures training. The lives of residents are further enriched through programs that range from home ownership counseling to computer training and advanced education.

Through partnerships with various community entities, DHA is able to bring a wealth of resources to those served. A prime example of the community working together is the development of the former tobacco plant known as The Golden Belt Center, an economic development service entity housing employment related programs.

DHA's efforts are changing the face of assisted housing. One initiative is to more seamlessly blend its properties into the fabric of the surrounding community. Woodridge Commons, Edgemont Elms Apartments, Northtowne, the award-winning Preiss-Steele Place, apartments for seniors, Kerrwood II for new homeowners, and Laurel Oaks, the newest public housing complex, all represent this new face.

Through its $35 million HOPE VI Revitalization grant, DHA is demonstrating its commitment to helping enhance Durham's quality of life. HOPE VI centers on the redevelopment of a ninety-six block area into increased affordable rental and home ownership opportunities within a mixed income context. The grant will also support such programs as child care assistance, job placement and life skills training.

Although the road ahead is filled with challenge, the Durham Housing Authority will continue to pursue positive change. "We will never be content with where we are; we'll always be looking for a better place to go" says Tabron. "Our objective is to make Durham as good a place to live as possible for everyone. We do that one household at a time!"

Below: J. Alice B. Hayswood and Warren Lipscomb enjoy the feeling of independence they get from living in Forest Hills Heights in downtown Durham. Open since 1981, the housing community consists of fifty-five units for seniors living on limited income. Right: The newly constructed Laurel Oaks community provides the foundation for participants of the family self-sufficiency program. In this program, family members learn the skills they need to become successful homeowners.

Tim Wright—Both

With the revitalization of downtown Durham, the city's center has become a unique blend of tradition and modernization. More than one million square feet of formerly unoccupied space is now home to restaurants, shops, upscale apartments, and business space for corporations and entrepreneurs alike. While the decline of the tobacco industry spelled certain doom for some, the turn-of-the-century warehouses in downtown Durham have become the premier shopping experience in The Triangle. Brightleaf Square (far right) is a thriving shopping and dining district, filled with nationally renown restaurants, art galleries, and specialty shops of every sort. Nostalgic neon signs from Public's Hardware on Mangum, the Oyster Bar on Main and Gregson, and the Book Exchange on West Chapel Hill Street also bring back memories of days-gone-by.

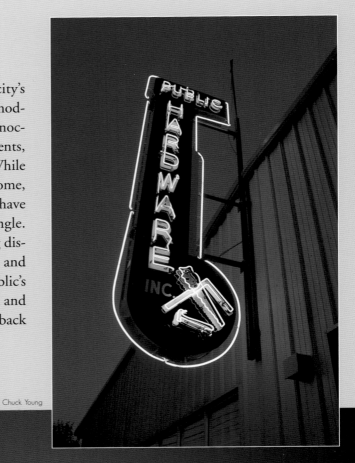

Chuck Young

Tim Wright

Chuck Young—All

Triangle Orthopaedic Associates, P.A.

Everyone deserves quality care for the aches and pains that life brings. For the residents of Durham and surrounding areas, that care is delivered by the dedicated professionals at Triangle Orthopaedic Associates, P.A.

For patients with musculoskeletal and pain problems, these physicians provide relief through programs involving physical and rehabilitative medicine,

occupational therapy, chronic pain management, and orthopaedic surgery when needed. These high-quality orthopaedic services and ancillary programs extend beyond the metropolitan area to eight satellite offices in smaller cities that make care more convenient for area residents.

Regardless of ability to pay, patients have always been treated with dignity at Triangle Orthopaedics. Even patients needing same-day care are seen by physicians so devoted to their work that they often remain after hours. That dedication to medical excellence has helped Triangle Orthopaedics grow from a small partnership formed nearly one half century ago to an association of more than fifty professionals that

The future home of Triangle Orthopaedic Associates, P.A. is a sixty-five-thousand-square-foot state-of-the-art musculoskeletal center. The new facility houses all of the amenities necessary to provide high quality care and excellent service to patients suffering from musculoskeletal disorders.

Bill Touchberry

Ken Hawkins

include orthopaedists, physiatrists, a behavioral psychologist, physician assistants, nurse practitioners, physical therapists, and athletic trainers.

Trained in the nation's best residency programs, these orthopaedic associates each hold a broad range of experience in all types of musculoskeletal problems and injuries. Many of the associates also have fellowship-added qualifications. Specialties within the group include adult and joint reconstruction; sports medicine; pediatrics, including an emphasis on scoliosis and cerebral palsy; therapies for problems of the spine, foot, and ankle; and surgeries of the shoulder, knee, and hand.

The group's specialists also include an acupuncturist providing complementary treatments as well as "The Golf Doctor™," a former golf professional and preeminent authority on shoulder and elbow disorders.

By combining their expertise to create multi-disciplinary treatments, these physicians have formed the Triangle Regional Interdisciplinary Pain Program (TRIPP), which brings relief to injured workers through chronic pain management.

(l-r) The Executive Committee of Triangle Orthopaedic Associates, P.A., is comprised of Drs. Thomas A. Dimmig, William J. Mallon, Robert J. Wilson, Peter W. Gilmer, David T. Dellaero, Ralph A. Liebelt, and Edwin T. Preston. The decisions of these professionals guide the practice in delivering excellence in service.

But rather than simply treat disorders, Triangle Orthopaedics encourages preventative measures. In addition to a Wellness Center that promotes healthy lifestyles, the group's ergonomic specialists work with individuals and corporations to prevent work-related injuries.

With a new sixty-five-thousand-square-foot, state-of-the-art main campus in Independence Park, Triangle Orthopaedics has now brought together its entire sub-specialty practice under one roof. The facility is adjacent to Durham Regional Hospital and the Davis Ambulatory Surgical Center, two of the numerous hospitals that Triangle Orthopaedics physicians utilize.

Moving ahead technologically, the associates have recently partnered with the Austin-based @Outcome

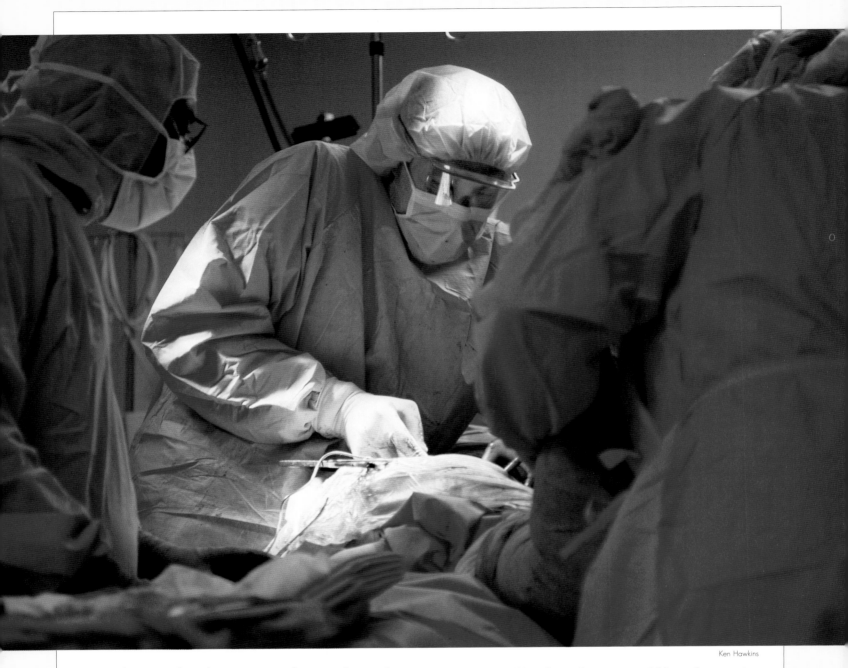

Ken Hawkins

to perform studies that measure the practice against benchmarks nationwide. And through the Triangle Orthopaedic Research & Education Foundation, the practice performs clinical research studies that bring cutting-edge therapies to patients.

Although it is a private practice, the association's interests lean toward academia. Its community initiatives often focus on education and include screenings, health fairs, and annual conferences addressing professionals in the fields of medicine and sports. Additionally, the associates distribute a helpful newsletter to primary care doctors who are often the first line of defense in musculoskeletal disorders. As concerned sports medicine professionals, Triangle Orthopaedic physicians can be found on the sidelines

Dr. Thomas A. Dimmig performs a total hip replacement in the North Carolina Specialty Hospital, of which Triangle Orthopaedic Associates is a part owner. Physicians in the practice utilize numerous hospital facilities throughout the region.

of games in every county they serve providing coverage for area sports teams. Their quality of care has earned these associates the position as team physicians for the Durham Bulls AAA Baseball Team.

By being responsive to patient needs and delivering care on a local basis, the specialists at Triangle Orthopaedic Associates, P.A. are improving the quality of life for the people of Durham and surrounding communities.

Today the century-old Union Grove United Methodist Church (right) has a congregation of thirty. "It's a warm, friendly church, and its focus is on worship and the sacraments," says Pastor Steve Hall, who leads the one Sunday morning service. Rev. Bennie C. Torian (below) leads the congregation at Greater Orange Grove Baptist Church on Roxboro Road.

Chuck Young—All

Chuck Young

The pristine water of Parkwood Lake is a beautiful aspect of the Parkwood Community. Recently annexed by the city, Parkwood's medium-priced homes have long attracted younger families and the more transient populace of the Research Triangle area. Years ago, when the lake's waters were down, Doris Schneider built an island on a portion of her property. Today, the island is a showcase of native flora planted by her and husband Jim Coke, a wildflower specialist. Together, they enjoy canoeing on the peaceful lake and caring for the island's plantings.

In the last few years, soccer has become the sport of choice for many in Durham. In 1996, the Durham Neighborhood Youth Soccer Association was formed and quickly gained the attention of inner-city youth. Soon, entire families joined in the activities and can still be seen on the sidelines cheering for their teams. In addition to the popularity of the sport among the area's youth, playing "futbol" is a passion brought from home for many of the city's Hispanic population. The formation of the city's Hispanic league created not only a chance for members to play, but also avenues for communication among non-English speaking members of the community. These Hispanic teams can be seen playing with great zeal in parks and fields around the city.

David Murray

Duke University

From its beginnings as a regional college, Duke University has grown into an institute known for its commitment to excellence. Today the name Duke is world-renown for distinction in academics, medical research, athletics, and community service.

The school was first established in a nearby community in 1838, later moving to Durham to become Trinity College. In 1924, the college became Duke University by provision of The Duke Endowment. Created by James Buchanan Duke, the endowment provided for expansion of facilities and academics and for the university to be named in honor of his father, Washington Duke.

Today the Duke University campus and medical centers employ more than 20,000 people, making it the largest employer in the city of Durham.

More than 10,000 students attend Duke in pursuit of undergraduate and graduate degrees in the arts and sciences, medicine, law, business, environment, and engineering. A renewed focus on curriculum now emphasizes arts and literature, civilizations, natural sciences and mathematics, and social sciences. And requirements in cross-cultural studies, scientific reasoning, and ethical inquiry help students understand the learning process while preparing them to fully participate in the world beyond graduation.

Duke's scholarly achievements impact the global community. Research performed by both students and faculty is bringing new understanding to issues affecting the land, public policy, and the human condition in countries around the world. The University and its health systems are internationally recognized for excellence and nearly one half of Duke's students participate in undergraduate studies abroad.

For many, the name Duke means outstanding intercollegiate athletics for both men and women. Although the men's basketball team lost its first game in 1906, today it borders on tradition to find the Blue Devils advancing to the Final Four. Duke teams are regularly placed among the nation's top ten and four Blue Devil coaches earned National Coach of the Year titles in the 1999-2000 season. The men's basketball team won the national championship in 2001.

Duke's dedication to making a difference extends its involvement in the community. Locally, the Duke-Durham Neighborhood Partnership Initiative is improving neighborhoods surrounding the campus through tutoring, safety programs, housing rehabilitation assistance, a wellness clinic, and more. Duke's medical professional training and patient care programs are bringing attention to underserved areas while educating youngsters about the importance of good health. And while Duke law students brought volunteer legal counseling to victims of Hurricane Floyd, environmental students began studying the storm's ecological aftereffects.

Duke students, faculty, and staff can also be found helping organizations that provide relief to members of the community and serving people with special needs such as hearing impaired children, specially challenged athletes, and HIV patients. These efforts for society have broadened the founder's aspirations by taking Duke University beyond its role as a center of learning to a position of leadership in community service.

When James B. Duke endowed Duke University in 1924, he specified that a coordinate college for women was to be established as a complement to the university. Formerly Trinity College, the East Campus served as the Woman's College from 1930 to 1972. Today it is home to several major departments and programs as well as First Year students at Duke.

Les Todd—Both

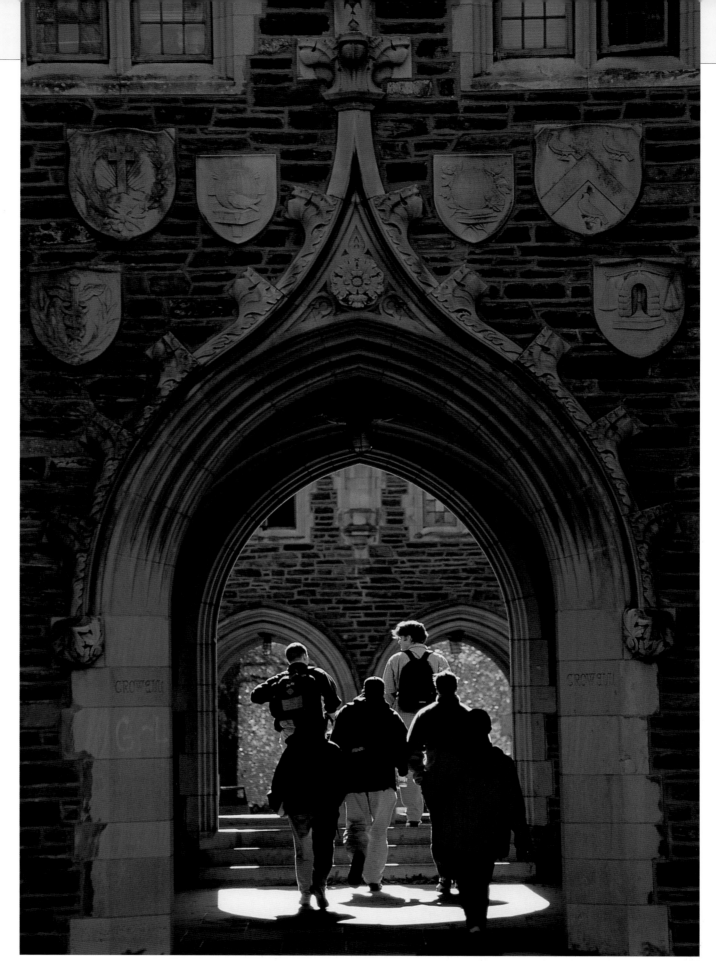

Every day, hundreds of students walk through the Crowell Arch on their way to classes on Duke's West Campus. This passageway lies beneath the soaring clocktower at the entrance to Crowell Quandrangle. From left to right, the six shields represent medicine, the Duke University seal, religion, biology, the Duke family coat of arms, and law.

Over in Orchard Park, a small group of trees receives the special attention of one long-time Durham resident. In his eighties, James Bradley cares for his special "pets" in what was once the garden of Hill House, home of Central Carolina Bank Founder John Sprunt Hill. The park and house are in Morehead Hill, once an elite Durham neighborhood that is now inhabited by a diverse residential population.

Tim Wright

Greg Foster

Although he is best known as a man of vision, those who know him say John Hope Franklin is also a man of great heart. Quite a statement for a man whose accomplishments could encompass three lifetimes. In addition to *From Slavery to Freedom*, his definitive 1947 work of the black experience in America, Franklin has authored a dozen books and is a 1995 recipient of the Presidential Medal of Freedom. Duke University honored the historian and civil rights leader by placing of portrait of him in the Gothic Reading Room of the Perkins Library. In addition, the university named the John Hope Franklin Research Center for African and African-American Documentation after its professor emeritus. Franklin is recognized in the world of botany as well. In 1996, the Phalaenopsis John Hope Franklin was named after this avid orchid grower and collector.

Durham Public Schools

Durham Public Schools serves 30,000 students in forty-four schools across Durham County. The system's overarching goal is that of continually increased student achievement, which has experienced a steady, upward trend since 1997.

Success has not occurred by accident. The system is committed to infusing programs and services of highest quality and innovation to provide students with a top-rate instructional experience. Magnet, year-round and lab schools, along with high school Centers of Specialization and International Baccalaureate programs provide a wealth of choices.

Some of the finest school facilities in the state of North Carolina can be found right here in Durham, largely as the result of two, $200 million-plus capital improvement plans, the first of which was completed in the mid-1990s, and the second slated for completion by 2008. All of the schools are fully "wired" for the Internet. From Web site development to digital portfolios to database analysis, Durham Public Schools offers the latest in technological instruction.

Much of the school system's success is directly linked with a very supportive community that is aware of its responsibility for providing resources—both monetary and human—toward this end. Business and community partners include some of the nation's leading corporations—GlaxoSmith Kline, IBM, Nortel and Verizon—as well as more than 200 mid- and small-sized businesses and community organizations. Local institutions of higher learning including Duke University, North Carolina Central University, Durham Technical Community College and the neighboring University of North Carolina at Chapel Hill, provide in-kind services such as professional development, tutors/volunteers, and technical assistance.

Durham Public Schools incorporates a variety of innovative learning environments—including magnet programs, Centers of Specialization, lab and year-round schools—to serve 30,000 students from Durham County. Since 1997 the district has experienced a steadily upward trend in student achievement due to a clear focus on high-quality instruction and effective professional development.

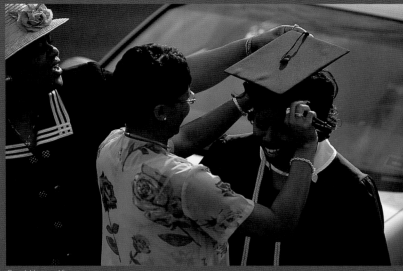

David Murray—All

It was a beautiful day for a celebration as nearly seven hundred graduates and family members filled North Carolina Central University's new O'Kelly-Riddick Stadium. Rousing cheers and joyful tears erupted from a crowd of graduates—many honored for their achievements, while others grateful for having made it to this eventful day. The 2001 graduation was also the last for Chancellor Julius Chambers, who retired following eight years of leadership. Today, James H. Ammons Jr. is at the helm of NCCU, dedicated to leading the university through the challenges of the future.

Driving along Farrington Road is a step back in time when approaching Patterson's Mill Country Store. A period billboard, vintage advertisements, and an old-time gas pump greet visitors to this two-story clapboard structure. Built in the 1870s, this reconstructed country store contains a doctor's office, a pharmacy, and one of the area's finest collections of mercantile, pharmaceutical, and tobacco memorabilia. Retired pharmacist Elsie Hudson Booker, in her seventies, can still be found in the pharmacy area of the store. Three brass cash registers from 1890 and penny candy-filled jars can be seen through the windows from the wraparound balcony.

Northgate Mall

There is a reason so many people find Northgate Mall an exciting place to shop. It's because this locally-owned mall is tuned in to what people of the region need.

Northgate Mall has been a family operation since its inception. When Durham-native W. Kenan Rand Jr. purchased the property back in the 1950s, it was a tobacco farm that he intended to use as the relocation site for his downtown Coca-Cola bottling plant. But upon further consideration, Rand realized the loca-

tion's retail potential and developed it into the Northgate Shopping Center.

A decade after the strip mall opened in 1960, plans were in the works to turn the community-based center into an enclosed mall. Today, Northgate Mall anchor tenants include Belk, Hecht's, and Sears as well as more than one hundred specialty shops offering everything from apparel to home furnishings to collectible gifts. The Mall Food Court is home to thirteen fast food operations, and has services at the

Ken Hawkins—Both

mall ranging from banking to photo processing to the BigFatWow with its free Internet access.

Virginia Rand Bowman, second generation of the mall family, oversees the mall's development and long range planning. Bowman has grown up with the family business. She carries on the family trait of being flexible in responding to the needs of tenants and shoppers with a strong administrative staff. Bowman has also led the mall through its fourth renovation in 2001, upholding the tradition that the center should constantly strive to provide the most up-to-date shopping environment for its customers.

Northgate Mall is considered to be a gathering place for the community. Shoppers often find the

Left: Soft seating throughout Northgate Mall makes shopping a comfortable experience. The mall's relaxing, family atmosphere stems from local ownership that understands what appeals to the people of the Triangle. Above: Carlyle & Co. is one of the many interesting shops to be found in Northgate Mall. With more than 160 local, regional, and national stores, the mall's variety offers something for everyone.

halls lined with such extras as motorcycle, boat and car displays, hybrid flowers, and fashion shows. The yearly raffle held for the Parade of Play Homes is an exciting event benefitting abused children. Child-related activities such as Peter Rabbit in Mr. McGregor's Garden, the holiday Northgate Express Train, and the Americana Carousel (complete with dragon) provide parents with healthy entertainment for their children. Parents also appreciate the annual Duke Safe Kid's Fair with its games, safety and prevention information, infant car seat installments, and Ident-A-Kid program. And the annual Community Service Fair brings together more than forty not-for-profit organizations.

The Northgate Mall Beach Party draws thousands to the roof of the parking deck. Meanwhile, the mall's fundraising efforts have helped the Durham County Habitat for Humanity build a home in a neighborhood just down the street from the shopping complex. It's these kinds of activities that represent the conviction of the people behind Northgate Mall to truly respond to the needs of their community and be supporters of the place they call home.

As members of the communities they serve, the officers of the Durham County Sheriff's Office take great pride in improving the quality of life in the county by working with citizens to ensure their safety and welfare. In recognition of the growing senior population in the area, the city of Durham's Sheriff's Office conducts a TRIAD program. Through TRIAD, officers work with elderly citizens to educate them about crime prevention and other programs with the sheriff's office. The program opens lines of communication between citizens and the

David Murray

department to help involve seniors in finding solutions for issues that concern their safety and well-being. Officers Ernie Mills Jr. and Walter McIntyre (above) visit with Albert McFail and Junior Thompson while they relax around a checkers game. The Durham Police Department is on a mission to improve the overall quality of life. More than 450 sworn police officers serve a city of 187,000 people, working in partnership with the city's leaders, residents, and agencies to build trust while reducing crime in the area. In order to maintain close contact with citizens and respond quickly when needed, uniformed bicycle officers patrol both the city's business and downtown areas, as well as the city park system.

Chuck Young

A visit to the Duke Homestead and Tobacco Museum is a step back in time. Costumed players in this living history museum reenact the early days of tobacco manufacturing, the product that built the Duke dynasty. Upon his return from service in the Civil War, patriarch Washington Duke sold the coveted Bright Leaf tobacco to the Union soldiers. With his children alongside, Duke processed the smoking tobacco on the family homestead and within a few years had built his third factory. The processes on display at the homestead today are the same used by Duke and his family. Youngsters Flannery Ronsick, Becky Woodrum, and Laura Woodrum (above) show how even the youngest Dukes were involved in building the family business. Also, Teresa Elliott and Angel Elliott cook the old-fashioned way using cast-iron cookware.

Bruce Feeley—Both

Cormetech, Inc.

The nation's need for power is growing. But along with keeping communities bright and safe, comes the need to safeguard the environment. That's where Cormetech excels.

Cormetech, Inc. manufactures selective catalytic reduction (SCR) catalysts. Installed in power and industrial plants, these catalysts can reduce up to 95 percent of harmful ozone polluting nitrogen oxide emissions by reducing them to water and harmless nitrogen. Nitrogen oxides are precursors to ground level ozone (smog) and acid rain.

Cormetech was founded in 1989 by Corning Incorporated employees who recognized the potential of the company's automotive emissions control technology applied to upcoming regulations for power plants. A worldwide search for a partner with experience in the SCR catalyst industry led the founders to Mitsubishi Heavy Industries, Ltd. and the formation of a joint equity company.

In 1991, Cormetech established its headquarters and a manufacturing operation in Durham. Soon after, the company secured contracts primarily in California, one of the nation's first states to adopt Cormetech's technology in complying with clean air regulations.

When that state's minimum requirements were met in 1995, Cormetech expanded its search for overseas contracts. The industry in the United States had stalled in the wake of debates between the federal government, states, and businesses over details associated with the new regulations. "We ended up running the equipment ourselves," says President and Chief Executive Officer Fred Maurer, recalling the company's reduced workforce days. "But it helped us better understand our processes. We received many orders for products that were different from our typical products. Although difficult at the time, the process and product understanding that came from that experience jump-started a current strength of Cormetech— continuous product improvement."

David Murray

Left: (l-r) Cormetech's Project Engineer Mark Barger discusses project details with Plant Manager Ed Brewer of Carolina Power and Light's Mayo Steam Plant. Partnerships with customers permit Cormetech to provide answers from planning through maintenance beyond installation. Right: President and CEO Fred Maurer (center), flanked by Operations Associates (l-r) Vickie Barnes and Rafael Estrada, with the new 2.1 millimeter pitch product. Cormetech's technically-minded staff is driven beyond understanding existing products to create new innovations for the industry.

David Murray

Constant change is a good thing for Cormetech's clientele. "As we're successful in introducing a new or improved product, we pass on the cost reductions that evolve from it to our customers," says Co-founder and Senior Vice President Reda Iskandar.

Since catalyst design requires constant updates, that forward vision is ideal for customers like the Tennessee Valley Authority (TVA), a $68 million contract Cormetech secured in 1998 following the resolution of the long-running emissions standards debate. Most contracts involve supplying multiple SCR systems to multiple units for natural gas and coal-fired power producers. By the year 2005, Cormetech's catalysts will be installed removing thousands of tons of nitrogen oxides (NOx) annually.

Clients with multiple units appreciate Cormetech's practice of forming an alliance to benefit from value-added services. "We're not just making the product, selling it, shipping it, and then walking away," says Iskandar. "Our alliances will go on for decades. We will walk with our clients step-by-step and help address issues and introduce improvements to the product that will constantly enhance the performance of their systems and reduce the cost of compliance."

As a show of commitment to the economic development of the TVA region, Cormetech opened a second plant in Cleveland, Tennessee in 2000. For years, Cormetech has been involved in workforce development issues, helping to form the Durham Workforce Partnership and supporting an apprenticeship program that provides job exposure for local high school students. The company has been recognized twice for its workforce improvement efforts.

Today, Cormetech—and the industry—are making great advances for the benefit of both people and the environment. "It's easy to get people excited about working with Cormetech," says Maurer, "because what they see is a product that really helps everybody."

Chuck Young

David Murray

Left: The installation of Cormetech's SCR catalyst in Georgia Power Company's Plant Bowen will enable the power generating company to reduce its nitrogen oxide emissions by hundreds of tons annually. Above: Lab Specialist Miguel Watkins guides Joel McKee through the High School Apprenticeship Program. Cormetech helped start the program, which has been vital in getting young people interested in the fields of technology and manufacturing.

David Murray—Both

Seafood, steak, and one of the Triangle's most renowned sushi bars are just some of the fares found under one roof at George's Garage. Housed in a converted supermarket, George's Garage is part of the happenings in the Ninth Street neighborhood. A bakery and market with prepared dishes round out the menu choices, and the bar is one of Durham's favorite night spots.

Tim Wright

Duke Children's Hospital & Health Center provides comprehensive health care for children from birth through young adulthood. In a new and colorful setting that includes a five-story atrium with aquarium, Duke's caring physicians and staff provide services ranging from routine immunizations to the most advanced medical care available for devastating childhood illnesses. Duke Children's researchers are also responsible for groundbreaking investigations that pave the way for treatments and cures of diseases such as pediatric HIV/AIDS and leukemia. Duke Children's is the largest charity health care provider in the state for children, providing more than $42 million in unreimbursed medical care in a single year's time.

Duke University Medical Center

From innovative preventive programs to advanced specialty services, Duke University Medical Center offers some of the world's finest health care.

Duke is consistently ranked among the top hospitals in the country; many of its more than 1,100 faculty physicians are nationally ranked among "The Best Doctors in America." Their guidance draws some of the nation's most promising students to the Duke University School of Medicine.

Duke is also world-renowned for "bench-to-bedside" biomedical research that provides Duke patients with access to the very latest therapies. Duke's research teams are credited with significant advances in human genetics and pharmaceutical development, and in the treatment of cancer, heart disease, AIDS, Alzheimer's and Parkinson's diseases, diabetes, and rheumatoid arthritis.

Duke's multidisciplinary clinical programs span the full spectrum of health care specialties. Physicians work closely with nurses, physical and occupational therapists, social workers, nutritionists, and other practitioners to provide customized treatment for each patient. Duke also offers extensive patient support and community education programs, as well as cultural services designed to meet the needs of international patients.

Duke University Medical Center is the cornerstone of Duke University Health System, a fully integrated network of health care facilities and providers. The Health System's partners include two area hospitals, ambulatory surgery centers, home infusion services, skilled nursing care, and hospice—each devoted to delivering quality, compassionate care.

Chris Hildreth

Below: Duke University Hospital (which includes the McGovern-Davison Children's Health Center, seen at left) was named as the Triangle's #1 hospital in terms of overall quality, reputation, and caregiver excellence in the 2000 Consumer Choice Awards. Left: Patients receive round-the-clock world-class care at the hospital, hub of Duke University Health System.

Les Todd

From basketball to golf, from rowing to swimming, from tennis to track, the women athletes of Duke University consistently excel in their sports. In 2001, the women's Blue Devils lacrosse team advanced to the NCAA Tournament for a fourth consecutive year.

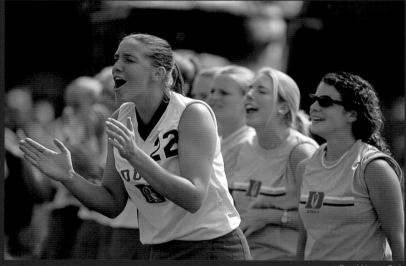

David Murray—Both

AW North Carolina, Inc.

At AW North Carolina, quality is more than a word, it is a way of life.

A subsidiary of Aisin AW Co., Ltd. of Japan, AW North Carolina manufactures automatic transmission components for Toyota Motor Manufacturing Company. Ensuring quality production in this plant begins with a team-based working environment that fosters respect and appreciation. Team members contribute ideas to operations by blending American creativity with the Japanese philosophy of *Kaizen*, or "always improving."

As an excited new member of the Durham community, AW North Carolina has demonstrated its intent to help the area prosper by developing a quality workforce through significant contributions to local technical colleges and school-to-career programs.

Although the company has purchased helmets for the local volunteer fire department, its proactive safety measures seek to eliminate the chance of them being used at the plant. The issue of workplace safety is a common topic at daily team meetings and the company employs both a safety, environmental, and health coordinator, as well as an occupational health nurse.

AW North Carolina is committed to maintaining environmental integrity as well. In addition to the lake occupying a portion of the company's 123-acre property, a tree is planted in celebration of each significant event at the facility. These trees stand as solid symbols of the culture at AW North Carolina—a work environment that promotes growth.

AW North Carolina is known for its advanced technology and equipment. Many of its components are manufactured on state-of-the-art equipment, such as this 2,300-ton AIDA press.

Blake Design

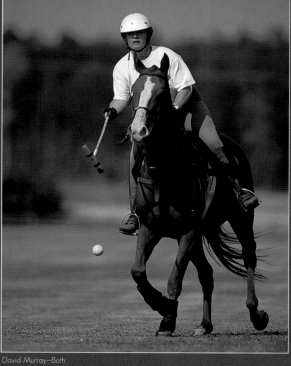

David Murray—Both

Every other Sunday, throughout the spring and fall months, the thundering of hooves and the thwack of the ball can be heard in Rougement. That's when members of the Chukker Downs Polo Club hold their matches at one of only two fields in the state. The polo field is part of the 110-acre Crystal Downs Farm, which specializes in dressage training.

Durham is a city of diverse cultures that is perhaps nowhere more apparent than at the annual Greater Durham International Festival. Live music, multicultural performers, and cultural displays are just a few of the fascinating features of this springtime event. Roaming entertainers and face painting are two activities for the younger set in the Kids Zone of the festival, and the International Food Market offers tastes from around the world.

Bruce Feeley

CrossComm, Inc.

With the immense amount of information on the Internet, the professionals at CrossComm, Inc. have what it takes to make a web site stand out. "We give our clients a distinctive image by developing strong creative solutions that demand to be noticed," says President and CEO Don Shin.

While CrossComm's full spectrum of services range from concept development to search engine optimization, its specialty is Internet multimedia—interactive animated interfaces, audiovisual web presentations, and Internet video.

CrossComm sites exhibit a rare quality—a balance of aesthetic beauty and practical functionality—that brings power and creativity to business web sites like

CrossComm, Inc. is the vehicle to accomplish the vision of President and Founder Don Shin. That dream is to make an impact on the community in many ways, primary of which is to equip underprivileged communities with information technology skills and resources.

the Duke University Eye Center (www.dukeeye.org). "This site has a lot of multimedia gems. For example, we used interactive panoramic technology to let users 'walk through' the building. We also simulated the Center's Touchable Art Gallery for the vision-impaired by interactively rotating art pieces 360 degrees," explains Shin. Users can also experience this blend of art and technology on The Ciompi Quartet site (www.ciompi.org), with its online audio selections, and on the King's Park International Church web site (www.kpic.org), which contain video presentations and audio sermons.

CrossComm creates individualized solutions for clients by striving to understand their business goals and objectives. "Our objective is to produce results for an organization," says Shin, "whether in the form of increased publicity for a non-profit, increased revenue for a business, or by creatively discovering ways that Internet technology can change the way work is done within an organization."

Chuck Young

Bruce Feeley

Not only are CrossComm's creations visually striking, they are also very easy to use—factors conducive to the Internet needs of The Greater Durham Chamber of Commerce (www.durhamchamber.org). "In a technology-focused city like Durham it is important for the Chamber to be able to convey a tech-savvy image to our online users," says David J. Neill, vice president of research for the Chamber. "CrossComm has an impressive track record of making the best in web technology work for companies like ours in a style that is still user-friendly to our wide audience."

Originally from Michigan, Shin founded the company while attending Duke University. With its formation, he began fulfilling his enduring interest in merging communication arts with information technology. However, he hopes that his expertise will allow him to accomplish loftier goals. As a young man, I had a religious experience that changed my

To see the diverse staff at CrossComm is to see the face of Durham. (l-r) David Hobbet, Beena Mathew, Robert Lowry, Don Shin, Omar Clinton, Shara English, and Carter Corker.

life," says Shin. "As a Christian, I realized I had a life-long mandate and calling to help the people and communities around me...so I want my company to play an integral part in the city's future successes."

Mindful of its philanthropic role in the community, CrossComm has produced a pro bono site for Duke Children's Hospital & Health Center (www.dukechildrens.org). "Creating a web presence was something we had wanted to do for quite some time, but we lacked the resources," says Katie Butler, public relations manager, stressing her delight in CrossComm's contribution to modernizing the online image of this state-of-the-art medical facility.

Shin's efforts to contribute to the community's success include positioning his company to address issues like future career opportunities for Durham's inner city children. "I want to eventually start an education center that will impart communication arts, information technology, and entrepreneurial skills to the next generation of Durham," he envisions. "And I look forward to CrossComm playing a prominent role in rallying the businesses of Durham behind these community efforts. Of course, I realize that big dreams often take big resources but I aim to learn all I can about how to acquire the resources that will make my life's goal a reality."

Right: The staff at CrossComm willingly shares its knowledge to help others in need. CrossComm's people train the staff at the Durham Rescue Mission so that they, in turn, can equip people who come to the facility with the skills they need to secure job opportunities. **Below:** CrossComm's talent truly lies in its ability to convey the client's message via electronic imagery. The uplifting atmosphere at Duke Children's Hospital will naturally be reflected in the web site as well.

Bruce Feeley

Bruce Feeley

With its roots stemming from a small Vermont town in the 1930s, the American Dance Festival has grown into the largest modern dance festival in the world. Each year, dance companies, choreographers, and students converge on the city to participate in more than a month of seminars, classes, and performances, all geared toward learning and celebrating the art of modern dance.

Bruce Feeley—Both

Hundreds of the area's youth participate in the national pastime each summer as part of the Durham Bulls Youth Athletic League. Through the efforts of Assistant Coach Donnie Weeks young athletes like Denzel Gooch (above) learn to enjoy the sport. Denzel is one of twelve members of the Dillard's Bar-B-Que team of six to eight year olds. In 2000 the team went undefeated. Head Coach Derrick Best promotes good sportsmanship and school academics to all his team members. Not only does he encourage good grades, he works with parents to resolve behavior issues that may potentially interfere with a student's success.

Bruce Feeley

Cardinal State Bank

In the wake of a sea of mergers among North Carolina's banks in the latter 1990s, two veterans of the Durham banking community decided to form a bank the people of the area could call their own. Their determination led to the formation of Cardinal State Bank, a full-service community bank that now operates from their branch on Westgate Drive. Plans include expansion of their branch network before the years end.

John Mallard and Harold Parker are the visionaries behind this new financial institution. In addition to their combined fifty years of banking expertise, they share a keen insight into the community's needs as natives of the area.

These traits helped bring together more than a dozen business, civic, and professional leaders from Durham and Chapel Hill, who joined the two in organizing the bank. More than 1,275 area residents joined in making the bank a reality by purchasing in excess of $14 million of common stock in an initial public offering.

Cardinal State Bank's local ownership provides product offerings that are ideally suited to the needs of its individual and commercial clientele, but what differentiates this bank is its quality of service. Personalized attention is the bank's competitive stance and deposits made here are invested in the local community.

In time, the bank's growth will undoubtedly include additional products and services. But for now, Cardinal State Bank is confident in its role as a community bank that is making a difference in North Carolina.

Like the Magic Wings Butterfly House at the North Carolina Museum of Life and Science, Cardinal State Bank is a vital thread in the Durham fabric. Both are guided by leaders who hold a strong sense of community pride. (Seated l-r) Bank President and CEO John Mallard Jr.; Director Alice Sharpe; and Board Chairman George D. Beischer. (Standing l-r) Museum President and CEO Thomas H. Krakauer; Bank Director Dan Hill III; Executive VP and CFO W. Harold Parker Jr.; Executive VP and CCO A. Lewis Bass III.

David Murray

Chuck Young

David Murray

Chuck Young

Durham is a city that proudly supports the arts and its artists. Displays of that pride can be seen in the many murals throughout the city. The mural at the top can be found on Manbites Dog Theatre on Geer Street. The Old Hayti Community Mural (left), in the Heritage Square Shopping Center, is the largest one of the many murals throughout the city created by Artist Emily Weinstein. In addition to outdoor murals, Weinstein paints murals and portraits in the homes of patrons. The mural at bottom left can be found on Foster Street. Artist Edie Cohn created the mural on the wall of the Durham Food Co-op (above) on West Chapel Hill Street. The colorful scene conveys the diversity of Durham in the shoppers at a farmer's market.

Chuck Young

Eisai Company, Inc.

When company leaders of Tokyo-based Eisai Co., Ltd. went looking for a site in the United States for a new pharmaceutical research and manufacturing facility, they found the people and activities at Research Triangle Park (RTP) to be the perfect fit. In 1997, that search culminated in the opening of Eisai Inc.'s state-of-the art pharmaceutical production and pharmaceutical and analytical research and development facility. As part of a rapidly growing international research-based pharmaceutical company, Eisai Inc. is the comprehensive U.S. pharmaceutical operating arm of its parent, Eisai Co., Ltd.

A highly skilled workforce at the RTP facility oversees the manufacture and packaging of two Eisai products: Aricept® (donepezil hydrochloride), for persons with Alzheimer's disease; and Aciphex® (rabeprazole sodium), for relief of gastroesophageal reflux disease.

Meanwhile, the RTP Pharmaceutical and Analytical Research and Development division contributes to providing Eisai with a fully integrated research and development function in the United States, complementing the company's drug discovery research at the Eisai Research Institute of Boston in Andover, Massachusetts, and its clinical research in Teaneck, New Jersey. Using formulation research, analytical chemistry, microbiology science and clinical supply manufacturing, the RTP team develops formulations for chemical compounds that move these potential therapies from the discovery function to clinical development, where they are administered to healthy volunteers and patients. This group also performs

Pharmaceutical and Analytical R&D staff contribute to the development of important, new medicines at Eisai, Inc's state-of-the-art facility at RTP.

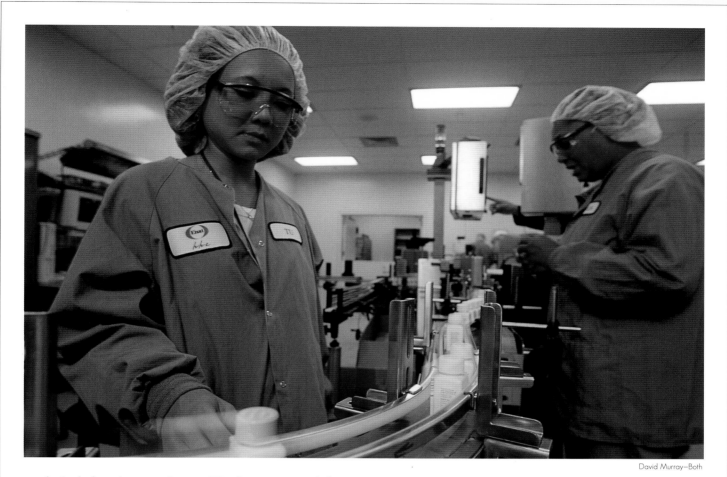

David Murray—Both

analytical chemistry testing on Eisai's commercial drug products to ensure conformity to established standards.

Eisai Co., Ltd. is a research-based *human health care* company with a network of research and development facilities, manufacturing sites, and marketing subsidiaries located in more than 30 countries around the world. Each year, this $2.9 billion company invests approximately 15 percent of its annual sales revenue into research and development of products, many primarily focused on treating the chronic and debilitating diseases afflicting today's elderly population.

Established in 1941 by Toyoji Naito, a retired senior executive for a Tokyo-based pharmaceutical company, Eisai remains true to its founder's belief in supporting the community. More than 7,000 employees worldwide share the company philosophy of *human health care*, symbolized by the initials *hhc*, which can be found in the signature of health care pioneer Florence Nightingale. Simply put, Eisai's *hhc* mission is to make a meaningful difference in the lives of patients and the patient's family.

To help the company constantly meet its *hhc* goals both inside and outside the workplace, Eisai personnel

Top: Eisai's packaging staff take a great deal of pride and satisfaction in packaging high-quality products.

Bottom: Three years after opening, Eisai's Research Triangle Park facility was already adding administrative offices, laboratories, and manufacturing space to its 85,000 square feet. The additional 24,148 square feet will allow Eisai to add nearly one hundred employees to its original crew of eighty-five.

Chuck Young

Tim Wright

utilize "knowledge creation" activities to conceive, share and implement new ideas. As a responsible corporate citizen in North Carolina, the RTP site turns out individually and in force to donate blood, assist

Top Left: Each year, Eisai employees and their families participate in the 5K Memory Walk for the Eastern North Carolina Chapter of the Alzheimer's Association. With nearly sixty walkers, Eisai had the most members of any corporation in the area in 2000. Eisai's Aricept product treats patients afflicted with the disease.

Bottom Left: Every Christmas approximately thirty-three Eisai volunteers, like (l-r) Natasha Boykin and Kendra Moneyhan volunteer to ring bells to collect donations for the Salvation Army. The collections are used to purchase toys, food, and other items for needy families in the area.

Below: When the community learned that the Red Cross was critically low on blood supplies, an Eisai staff member coordinated blood drive efforts at the facility. With the Bloodmobile on site, more than three dozen employees donated blood.

battered women, gather food supplies for Freedom from Hunger, lead scouts, round up toys for the Marine Corps, and ring bells for the Salvation Army. When hurricane Floyd devastated eastern portions of the state, RTP employees boarded on a bus and rushed to Rocky Mount to provide relief. The company's financial support includes funding of The Salvation Army's Life Sufficiency Program, Durham Technical Community College's program for scholarships to Durham high schools, The Herald Sun's Newspapers-in Education, American Red Cross Disaster Relief, fundraising for Duke Childrens' Hospital, The Arc of Wake County, and the Carolina Classic. And as a whole, Eisai is a major participant in Memory Walks, an awareness and fundraising event developed by the Alzheimer's Association.

The future is bright for Eisai Inc. at RTP as the facility now employs more than 130 people, and this 85,000 square foot facility is already expanding by an additional 24,000 feet. The people and activities here will continue to play an important role as Eisai continues to focus on globalization of its products to address unmet medical needs worldwide.

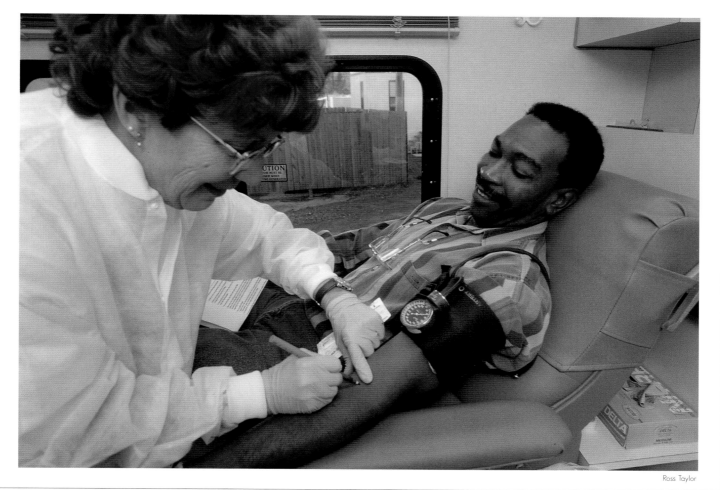

Ross Taylor

Tim Wright

Tim Wright

David Murray

King's Park International Church (bottom left and right) truly represents the diversity of Durham. Founded in 1981 near the UNC-Chapel Hill campus, King's has grown to establish numerous campus ministries, fifteen churches around the world, an overseas initiative, and youth ministries. Today, the church is building on its new property in Research Triangle Park. Temple Baptist Church (upper left) has been a downtown Durham landmark for more than one hundred years. But as its neighborhood has evolved, the church has seen a decline in membership. Thus, in 2000, Temple Baptist announced its move from the city center to Northwestern Durham, where Reverend Norman Harris will continue to lead all members of his congregation. When Deacon Joseph Blount Cheshire Jr. began walking twelve miles to conduct Sunday services for less than a dozen people back in 1878, little did he know the effect his dedication would have on the Durham community. Today, that small congregation has grown to more than eight hundred organized as St. Philip's Episcopal Church (below). This beautiful Main Street church is marked by a bell tower, which rises high above its vaulted ceiling.

David Murray

C.T. Wilson Construction Co., Inc.

Effective, upfront communication delivers a quality product and saves money for everyone involved. It has been the secret behind a half century of exemplary buildings and satisfied clients at C.T. Wilson Construction Co., Inc.

From planning to completion, every C.T. Wilson Construction project involves constant communication between the principal parties involved. Project managers combine knowledge and experience with the latest scheduling and cost-controlling software to provide personalized service through each phase of the process.

"We believe every student who comes out of the education system here needs work experience, whether that be an internship, a summer job, or a shadowing experience," says Chuck Wilson, who leads his management team by example in service on area advisory boards for the school system.

Local ownership and effective communication between employees also contributes to project success. Most of the company's projects are within a sixty-mile radius of Durham, and President and Owner C.T. "Chuck" Wilson believes everyone has something to contribute. "We listen to people and we put good ideas into action," he says. "We have found that two or three people working on a problem always come up with a better solution than just one person, and we incorporate that into our culture."

Through C.T. Wilson's on-line project management tool, information exchange has reached a new level of sophistication. Accessed via the company's web site, the tool provides all parties with instant information on their project's status and allows for timely and efficient resolution of any issue.

The C.T. Wilson standard of quality can be seen in new buildings as well as renovations of complicated

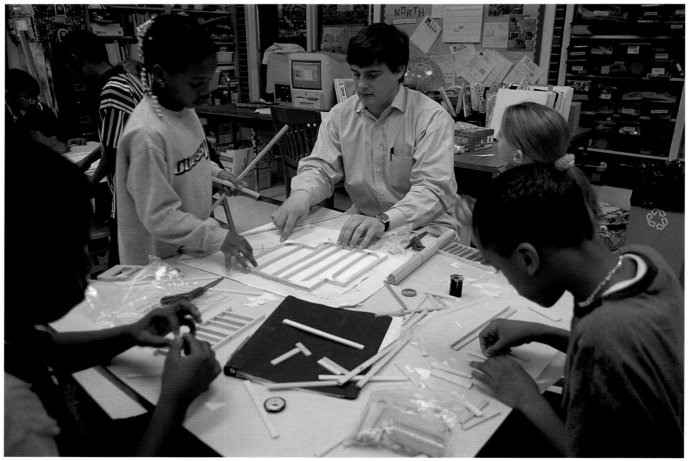

Tim Wright—Both

and sophisticated structures throughout central North Carolina. The company's portfolio includes healthcare facilities and research laboratories, commercial and government office buildings, educational and athletic facilities, and churches and industrial plants. C.T. Wilson services range from comprehensive general contracting to development for any portion of a project from preliminary budgeting to design and construction.

The company prefers working with clients who share common values. "We like to work with people who have a passion for the end product," says Wilson, who qualifies that outcome as a building that functions to the owner's needs.

Employees must also feel that same enthusiasm for the end result. "We like to hire people who want to improve not only themselves but also the company," Wilson says. The company aids internal promotion efforts through apprenticeship and training programs. Management staff are also required to participate in continuing education programs and all employees

Owner and President Chuck Wilson oversees the company's operations both in the office and on the job site. Since most are within driving distance of Durham, Wilson is able to keep open the lines of communication that are so vital to the success of every job.

enjoy full benefits including a share in the profits.

For the C.T. Wilson management team, building goes beyond the structural elements. Many are involved in civic or cultural activities with a special emphasis on education as advisory board members with the area's school systems. As a strong proponent for education, Chuck Wilson helped organize the Durham Workforce Partnership, which brings together area educators and business leaders. Members of management are also active leaders in the Carolina Association of General Contractors.

As Chuck Wilson says, "It is just good business to treat people fairly," and the rewards of good business are the quality buildings that grace the Durham community.

Whenever the Durham Bulls are in town, you can count on record-setting attendance at their downtown athletic park. That's because this Triple A baseball team has been making history since 1902. Over the years, the team has survived dissolution, the Great Depression, and the fiery destruction of its stadium. The team won its first pennant in 1924 and began the first in a string of major league affiliations in 1933. Today, the Durham Bulls are the Triple A affiliate of the Tampa Bay Devil Rays in the International League. Wool E. Bull, the eye-flashing, snout-snorting, tail-wagging icon of the movie "Bull Durham," remained behind after filming to become the team mascot. Opened in 1995, the Durham Bulls Athletic Park now seats ten thousand fans.

Ken Hawkins—Both

100

Throughout the spring and summer months, downtown Durham springs to life on the last Thursday of each month when concerts on the Civic Center Plaza bring music and entertainment (bottom right) to people as part of the Durham Alive celebration. Mascot for the Bulls, "Wool E. Bull" livens up the spirit of the concert series by greeting L' Dominique McDaniel (below). And then of course there are various food and floral offerings by the friendly faces of Maggie Smoak and Dana Allen (bottom left).

FOX 50 WRAZ-TV

When television viewers in the Triangle want to be entertained, they know to turn to FOX 50. FOX 50 is the place to find all the best comedies and the best dramas, the NFL, NASCAR, and Major League Baseball—including the World Series. And seven nights a week, Triangle viewers can stay connected and catch up on all the day's events through the FOX 50 News at Ten.

FOX 50's studios are located in the impressive Diamond View Office Building, which overlooks the outfield action of the Durham Bulls Athletic Park, home of the Tampa Bay AAA affiliate Durham Bulls. Not only does FOX 50's state-of-the-art facility fea-

ture premier local production capabilities, but FOX 50 was one of the first stations in the country to begin broadcasting a digital television signal. Digital television has allowed FOX 50 to multicast Durham Bulls baseball on one of its digital channels, while continuing to broadcast its regular programming on another.

FOX 50 is locally owned and operated by Capitol Broadcasting Company, Inc. In addition to Capitol's considerable media holdings throughout North Carolina, this multi-faceted communications enterprise is also the proud owner of the renowned Durham Bulls Baseball Club.

Sharing CBC's philanthropic philosophy, FOX 50 takes its role as a community leader seriously. In addition to offering quality entertainment and sports programming, FOX 50 actively supports a multitude of initiatives that address issues important to the communities it serves.

Viewers know they can stay connected with the FOX 50 News at Ten Team (l-r) Dwayne Ballen, Lynda Loveland, Cullen Browder, and Leon Smitherman for the latest on what's happening in the Triangle and around the world.

Ken Hawkins

Chuck Young

FOX 50 increases public awareness of family-oriented activities through in-kind advertising and monetary contributions. FOX 50 is the official television sponsor of one of the nation's oldest cultural festivals, the Bimbé Cultural Arts Festival. Bimbé is a regional celebration that brings together musicians, artists, and dancers for a week of activities that concludes with a free outdoor concert.

FOX 50 is also an official media sponsor of Light Up Durham, a holiday extravaganza and parade. In addition to donated publicity and promotion, FOX 50 broadcasts the parade, which is hosted by the station's news personalities.

Other community initiatives FOX 50 actively supports include Special Olympics North Carolina, Prevent Child Abuse North Carolina, and The Aggie-Eagle Classic, the annual football grudge match between North Carolina A&T University and North Carolina Central University.

For its support of area organizations, FOX 50 has received both the Anvil of Caring Award from the Triangle United Way and the Silver Beaver Award

As the official television sponsor, FOX 50 proudly provides complimentary airtime to advertise the Bimbé Cultural Arts Festival and helps bring in attendees from around the region. The celebration brings a wealth of information and fun to the community.

from the Occoneechee Council of the Boy Scouts.

FOX 50 also boasts an award-winning creative department. Among its many recognitions are a South East Regional Emmy, Promax Gold and Silver Medallion Awards, and "Best of the Best" Awards from the North Carolina Association of Broadcasters.

The talented team of professionals at FOX 50 is guided by the strong leadership of Jim Goodmon, President and Chief Executive Officer of Capitol Broadcasting Company, Inc. A distinguished visionary, Goodmon is well known throughout the Triangle community as a leader who understands the importance of corporate involvement in a community's success.

That sense of pride extends to FOX 50's role as a responsible broadcaster focused on enhancing the quality of life for all the people of the Triangle.

FOX 50 is proud to be a part of the Durham community and is committed to providing a quality mix of entertainment, sports and news programming, while at the same time continuing its tradition of positive community partnerships.

Right: FOX 50 supports Light Up Durham, a holiday extravaganza that includes the Durham Holiday Parade and the Light Up Durham fireworks finale. Below: FOX 50 broadcasts from this state-on-the-art digital facility which overlooks the outfield of the Durham Bulls Athletic Park.

Kevin Seiffert

Herald-Sun

Chuck Young

For four days and nights each year, Durham filmgoers have the opportunity to indulge their documentary desires in the DoubleTake Documentary Film Festival. The annual festival is international in scope, showcasing both new films and videos, as well as noted past documentaries. Screenings take place throughout the event in the beautifully restored Carolina Theatre and the Durham Arts Council theater. Panel discussions, workshops, and question and answer sessions help to stimulate discussion of both film content and the art of documentary filmmaking itself. And through informal sessions, an opening night gala, and nightly gatherings, fans and filmmakers can come together and share new ideas about the intriguing world of the documentary.

One day soon, walkers, joggers, bikers, and more will be able to traverse a path from the Durham Bulls Athletic Park in downtown Durham to New Hill Road in western Wake County. This is the projected route of the American Tobacco Trail, a thirty-mile Rails-to-Trails project in the Triangle area. The project is the work of the Triangle Rails-to-Trails Conservancy, Inc., an organization dedicated to preserving this local railroad corridor for use as a recreational trail and possible future transportation system. The first segment of the trail opened in 2000, spanning from Hillside High School to the Bulls park. A year later, on National Trails Day, this 5K race took place on the same section of the trail.

Chuck Young–Both

M&F-Mechanics and Farmers Bank

Since its opening in 1908, Mechanics and Farmers Bank (M&F) has remained devoted to the mission of its founders to promote economic development within the communities it serves and help its customers achieve their financial dreams.

That vision has earned M&F Bank the title as the state's oldest black-controlled bank and one of the most profitable in the nation. But today, as the world becomes more integrated, the role of this community bank is changing. "M&F Bank is here to serve all of the people of a community and not just one segment," says Lee Johnson Jr., president and chief executive officer of M&F Bancorp, Inc., the bank's holding company. "Regardless of their background or ethnicity, we want all people to have an opportunity to become a part of this institution and utilize the services that we have."

M&F Bank was chartered in 1907 by a group of businessmen led by R.B. Fitzgerald, a prominent Durham brickyard owner, whose bricks were used to build major Durham area businesses and churches. Its profitability record has been a consistently strong one with resources growing from $20,869 in 1908 to approximately $160 million today. In addition to its headquarters in Durham, M&F now has eight branches in Durham, Raleigh, Charlotte, and Winston-Salem.

Historically, M&F's reputation has been one of helping black homeowners and entrepreneurs realize their dreams. But beyond personal and business loans, M&F offers a full range of conventional products from savings accounts to certificates of deposit. More recently, M&F has answered the needs of a broader community with automated teller machines, debit cards, telebanking, extensive electronic services, internet banking, and a comprehensive web site. Additionally, the corporate office in Durham was recently relocated in a strategic move for current space needs and future potential growth.

Over the years, M&F has been a significant corporate neighbor. "We feel that as a good corporate citizen and member of the community, it's our responsibility to give back," says Johnson. "We try to do whatever we can in supporting the various institutions and organizations in spirit and in deed."

David Murray

M&F is an undisputed leader in mortgage lending. While the bank built a reputation as a lender to the under-served African-American community, today's M&F serves homebuyers from every walk of life.

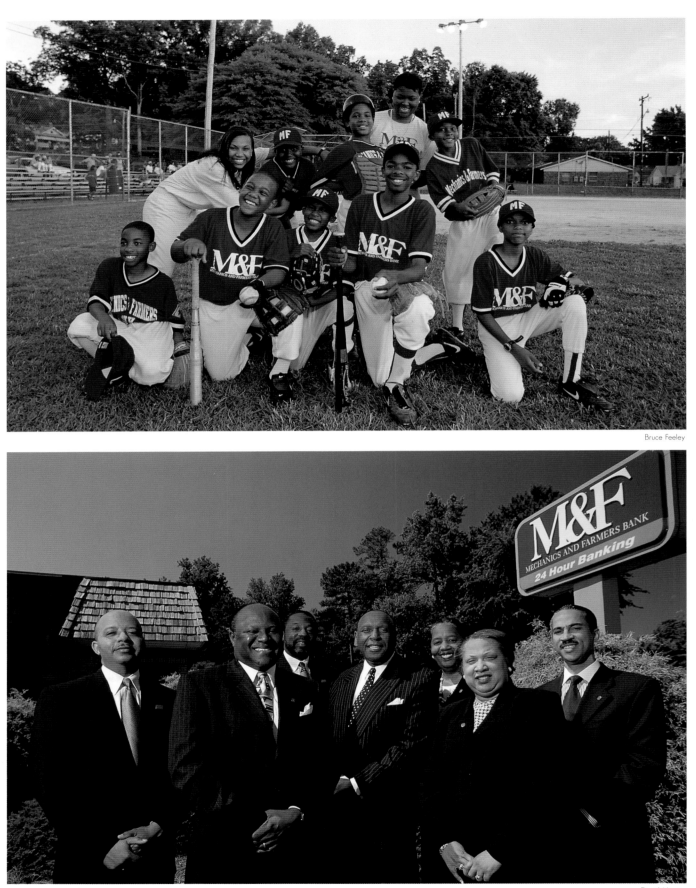

Bruce Feeley

David Murray

Top: M&F encourages its personnel to be active in the community. For some, time away from the bank is spent with the youngsters in the Durham Bulls Youth Athletic League. Above: Strong leadership has been a pivotal force in the success of M&F. As the future unfolds, its leaders will continue to guide it on a path to make it the area's leading community bank.

Bruce Feeley

M&F supports education for students at all grade levels. It was instrumental in helping nearby Shaw University overcome severe financial difficulties and it also supports programs that recognize the accomplishments of students and expose them to the world of business. The donation of its former Fayetteville Street branch to a local foundation means Durham will soon have a museum of the Hayti district history. And in 2000, the state recognized M&F for its monetary, in-kind, and volunteer contributions to the arts and humanities.

M&F has been repeatedly recognized for its banking accomplishments as well. Twice it has been named Bank of the Year by Black Enterprise magazine, and for forty-three consecutive quarters M&F has been awarded a five star rating for safety and soundness from Bauer's BankRater, a sentiment echoed by Veribanc, Inc.'s Blue Ribbon Bank™

Organizations like the Durham YMCA benefit from the bank's leadership talent. M&F personnel serve on boards of directors, as trustees for educational facilities, and as active participants in community civic, religious, and political organizations.

commendation. M&F's strength also earned it a place in Money magazine's 1988 survey of the Top 175 Safest Banks in the country and one of five in North Carolina.

For its future, M&F is exploring product offerings that will secure its place as a comprehensive financial services center. But above all, this community bank knows that building relationships are the key to a successful future for itself and its customers. "All money is green," says Johnson. "The major advantage we have is the ability to give quality service with a personal touch."

Dr. LeRoy T. Walker, Jr.

Frank A. DePasquale

Tim Wright—Both

The Triangle's cultural heritage is deeply enriched by the contributions of the Hayti Heritage Center. Visitors to the center will find a wealth of artifacts and visual arts on display as well as a dance studio and community meeting space. Exhibitions also include traditional and contemporary art by African-American artists known throughout the area and the nation. Operated by the St. Joseph's Historic Foundation, the center is located in the Hayti community, an area historically known for one of the most successful African-American business and marketplaces in the nation. A variety of activities presented by the Foundation each year include the Spirit of Hayti Awards Ceremony and Gala (above). This black-tie event honors leaders from Durham. Here, city mayor protem Howard Clement III (left), visits with many of the guests who have made great contributions to the arts and historic preservation on local and national levels.

In the 1920s, a sound arose from Durham that would resound over the city until this day. That sweet echo is the Piedmont Blues, the essence of the Bull Durham Blues Festival. This annual event features Blues notables from across the country who come to join in the range of instrumental music and songs that stem from African folk music.

Bruce Feeley—Both

Washington Duke Inn & Golf Club

In Durham, the Duke family name has long been synonymous with distinction. Following early successes in the tobacco industry, Washington Duke and his family gained worldwide attention for their achievements and philanthropic endeavors. Today the tradition of excellence continues in the superior service and Southern hospitality offered by the Washington Duke Inn & Golf Club. Located on the campus of Duke University, which was named in honor of the family patriarch, the Inn is Durham's finest hotel.

Duke family treasures adorning the Inn's public areas envelop guests in a world of heritage. This feeling of elegant comfort combined with warm, gracious hospitality contributes to the Inn's title to both the Mobil Four-Star and the American Automobile Association (AAA) Four-Diamond ratings.

The Inn's Fairview Restaurant has also received a AAA Four-Diamond Award. With its impeccable service, international specialties, seasonal fare, and a

Afternoon Tea is as elegant as it was in the days of gentility. Served in the Sunroom, this moment away from the rush of the day includes scones, sandwiches, and a variety of traditional sweets.

Chuck Young—Both

full selection of the finest wines, the Fairview is one of Durham's most elegant fine dining venues. For cocktails, conversation, and selections from the grill, many enjoy relaxing in The Bull Durham Bar. A visit to The 19th Hole snack bar includes a spectacular view of the golf course grounds. And the simpler traditions of yesteryear can be experienced at "Afternoon Tea" in the Sunroom.

Through continuous improvement of the Inn's facilities, guests are assured of the highest standards of quality and service. Decor inspired by the traditional English country inn, thick linens, and nightly turndown service provide special comfort for guests in each of the Inn's one hundred seventy-one rooms. Additional space and comfort can be found in the Inn's Homestead suite or any of six junior suites. And each room in the hotel offers voice mail and high-speed Ethernet connections to the Internet.

The luxurious grounds of the surrounding Duke University Golf Club are also a beautiful tribute to excellence. This eighteen-hole course has been recently redesigned by Rees Jones, son of the original designer Robert Trent Jones. In addition to the course, recreation at the Inn includes an outdoor pool overlooking the ninth fairway and a 3.5 mile walking or jogging trail winding through the lush Duke Forest.

The Inn's location near the Duke Medical Center and only minutes away from Research Triangle Park make it a premier gathering place for business and professional meetings and special events. From boardrooms to the Ambassador Ballroom to the Terrace on the Green, the Inn provides a warm, intimate setting for gatherings of any size. And the Inn's refreshing array of banquet menu selections that can be tailored to suit any need.

Like the regal symbol at its doors, the Washington Duke Inn and Golf Club holds a commanding presence on the university campus. Guests appreciate the sophisticated ambience of the Inn and its venues.

For visitors and residents of Durham who require elegant surroundings, exceptional service, and superior cuisine, the Washington Duke Inn & Golf Club provides an air of sophistication while retaining its Southern hospitality.

Chuck Young

More than 800,000 people in a thirteen-county area can tune in to WNCU for great jazz listening from DJ Larry Thomas (left). The public radio station broadcasts from North Carolina Central University on signal 90.7 FM. At North Carolina Central University, the Department of Art (below) offers programs that prepare students to teach art, pursue careers in the fine or communication arts, or use their talents on a variety of levels. The studio arts program concentrates on the mediums of painting, drawing, sculpture, printmaking, and ceramics. From observation and using life models, students in figure drawing classes study the human form. Ceramics classes (bottom right) begin with hand-building techniques and continue through wheel forming, glazing, and firing. Students with the talent may instead prefer to focus on sculpture.

Ken Hawkins—Both

North Carolina Central University's School of Education prepares students with the skills they need to be twenty-first century educators. In its new state-of-the-art building, the school incorporates the latest technologies in teachings while retaining the small class settings needed for one-on-one attention.

Cimarron Homes

Since 1982, Cimarron Homes has been fulfilling the dreams of Durham's first-time home buyers. With more than 2,000 quality homes to its credit, Cimarron has earned a solid reputation as "Durham's Home Builder."

Durham native and company president Craig Morrison heads up a team of housing professionals who understand the needs of area residents. "We are *the* local builder," says Craig Morrison, owner and president. "And we *only* build locally. It just comes natural to us."

In addition to entry-level neighborhoods like The Village at Horton Hills and Mabrey Landing, each offering quality construction and large homesites, Cimarron offers move-up choices in its portfolio: both Stagville at Treyburn and Oakbridge at Grove Park offer affordable golf course living options.

Delivering quality begins in the earliest planning stages, where Cimarron blends home-building expertise with state-of-the-art technology to produce appealing choices for the homebuyer. "We're very straightforward and methodical when it comes to managing cost," says Morrison. "That is then passed on to the buyer to deliver them good value." Standard options range from extra storage to energy efficient features to traditional elevations. And Cimarron backs up its quality with a ten-year residential warranty.

Cimarron has been repeatedly recognized for creating well-appointed, yet affordable homes. The company has received nearly three dozen Parade of Homes awards and twice been honored by the Triangle J Council of Governments. Furthermore, Morrison has won the "President's Award" from the National Association of Homebuilders and been named "Builder of the Year" three times, by the Homebuilder's Association of Durham and Chapel Hill.

Quality craftsmanship comes from a philosophy of continuous improvement. By building people through education, Cimarron has experienced an extremely low turnover rate. "We try to hire people who want to better themselves," says Morrison. "Without education they may look elsewhere for opportunity but we'd prefer that they learn and grow with us." Morrison and company also work with local schools to promote interest in the industry.

Cimarron Homes shares its expertise with the community in other ways. The company provided funding and crews to help build the city's Habitat for Humanity homes and three of Cimarron's Parade of Playhomes are bringing joy to neglected children from the area. "In a business sense we've been pretty successful and we've done it working in this community," says Morrison. "But we have a lot of fun being involved in reinvesting activities." The company is an annual sponsor of the Arthritis Foundation's annual golf tournament and has provided fund raising support for The American Heart Association, Muscular Dystrophy, and Hospice.

Although industry changes will continue to present challenges in offering the people of Durham high quality, affordable home choices, Cimarron Homes will remain committed to the task. "We like where we are," says Morrison. "They've been good to us here and we're not going anywhere."

Tim Wright—Both

(l-r) Superintendent Bill Beard, President Craig Morrison, and Assistant Superintendent James Anderson review blueprints at Marbrey Landing, one of the many Cimarron communities that offer value and quality in Durham.

Cimarron homes in Oakbridge at Grove Park offer residents quality, affordable golf course living. Amenities in this community include a pool, a clubhouse, tennis courts, a lake, and the Ron Garl Signature golf course.

David Murray

David Murray

Chuck Young

Five miles of walks and pathways meander throughout the Sarah P. Duke Gardens. Located on fifty-five acres on the Duke University West Campus, the gardens were begun with a $20,000 donation by the widow of Benjamin N. Duke, one of the university's founders. Today, that original bed of one hundred flowers has grown to encompass the Terraces, a selection of rose beds, perennials, a pergola, and fishpond; the Blomquist Garden of Native Plants, featuring a collection of plants native to the southeastern states; and the Culberson Asiatic Arboretum, dedicated to Asian plants.

Stubbs, Cole, Breedlove, Prentis & Biggs, P.L.L.C.

For more than a half century, one law firm has been an integral part of the Durham legal and civic landscape. Stubbs, Cole, Breedlove, Prentis & Biggs P.L.L.C. is the epitome of legal representation and commitment to the Durham community.

In 1932, Allston J. Stubbs began his law practice in Durham. For three decades, Mr. Stubbs developed a law practice concentrating on residential and commercial real estate transactions and representing banking and commercial institutions—areas of legal expertise that were strengthened when C. Thomas

(l-r) Darin Meece and Ike Breedlove greet Judy Lapeza at the firm's downtown offices. As spearheads of the downtown renewal efforts, the firm was one of the first businesses to purchase and renovate an historical building in the city's center.

Biggs and James A. Cole Jr. joined with him in the 1960s. This new partnership grew in the years that followed, maintaining an emphasis on real estate transactions and representation of banking institutions while broadening the practice into all areas of civil law and limited areas of criminal law.

Throughout its growth, Stubbs Cole has remained committed to the belief that rendering legal representation is about more than resolving a single issue, it is about building long-term relationships with clients. From buying a first home to dealing with the death of a family member, these attorneys believe in providing legal counsel for any matter arising in the lives of their clients.

The firm's current areas of practice include civil and criminal trial law with special emphasis in the areas of banking, business law, corporate, com-

David Murray

Below Left: Cynthia and John Marnell of Cynmar Designs, Inc. rely on the legal expertise of Attorney Dan Milam. His real estate savvy has helped the Marnells grow into a leading residential builder in the Triangle. Below Right: Clients like Craig Morrison (center) of Cimarron Homes appreciate the personal attention of Attorneys (l-r) Jon and Tom Biggs. The firm's members believe in building long-term relationships with clients.

David Murray—Both

This scope of expertise has earned Stubbs, Cole, Breedlove, Prentis & Biggs the trust and respect of major clients that range from regional banks and pharmaceutical distributors to real estate developers and builders.

The firm's commitment to excellence in legal representation is mirrored in its dedication to the Durham Community. With a considerable number of native residents among its membership, the firm is more than a provider of legal services, it is an investor in the Durham community. Stubbs, Cole was a leader in revitalization efforts in the city's center through the purchase and renovation of a historical downtown building that now serves as the main office for the firm.

mercial transactions, real estate, wills and estates, trusts, construction, bankruptcy, family law, and personal injury law. Among the firm's lawyers are certified mediators.

Traditionally, the firm has also demonstrated its commitment to service in the Durham area by

Bruce Feeley

David Murray

Above: Members of the firm, representing an average twenty-years experience, are: (seated, l-r) Ike Breedlove, Jim Cole, and Tom Biggs; (standing, l-r) Darin Meece, Jon Biggs, Terry Fisher, Dan Milam, and Rick Prentis. Left: In addition to attorney talent, the firm's on-site resources include professional support staff and full computer services. Here, Legal Assistant Joyce Slight works with Attorneys Terry Fisher and Rick Prentis on a case in litigation.

taking an active interest in community activities. In addition to board seats with numerous organizations, members of the firm have served as presidents of Triangle Hospice, Inc., the Durham Kiwanis Club, the North Durham Rotary Club, The Duke Durham Alumni Association, the Durham Jaycees, the Museum of Life and Science, and the Durham YMCA.

The firm's attorneys also maintain professional membership in the Durham County, North Carolina, and American Bar Associations; the North Carolina State Bar; the North Carolina Academy of Trial Lawyers; and the American Judicature Society. Members of the firm have served as Secretary-Treasurer of the North Carolina Bar Association and as Executive Secretary to a past Governor of the State of North Carolina.

When individuals, families, and businesses in Durham need help with the legal matters that affect their lives, they know they will receive fair, effective, and accessible legal representation from the professionals at Stubbs, Cole, Breedlove, Prentis & Biggs, P.L.L.C..

When the tobacco industry went bust and left vacant warehouses in its wake, Christian Laettner and Brian Davis (two former Duke basketball players) were joined by businessman Tom Niemann to help in the reformation efforts of downtown Durham. Today, Blue Devil Ventures is a community development company touted as a catalyst for revitalization through its West Village development. These loft-style rental apartments are housed in five tobacco warehouses built nearly a century ago by the American Tobacco Company and Ligget & Myers. Each retains the unique architectural components of the brick and wood warehouse with its expansive archways and massive windows.

David Murray

North Carolina Museum of Life and Science

Over one half century ago, Durham residents learned about nature by visiting a small trailside nature center. Today, the North Carolina Museum of Life and Science is a regional science and technology center renowned for its engaging hands-on exhibits and informal educational programs.

Visitors find interactive exhibits that invite experimentation and exploration both indoors and out-doors at the Museum. While permanent indoor exhibits include a thirteen-foot tornado, a full-scale Lunar Lander replica, and a virtual reality area, traveling shows throughout the year may bring an exploration of microbes or a chance to see the world through insect eyes. Visitors can handle snakes or hissing cockroaches in the Tree House Discovery Room.

Outdoors, visitors learn about domestic and wild animal species at the Museum's Nature Park and Farmyard. Keepers care for endangered red wolves, black bears, sheep, goats and birds. Loblolly Park with drums and water play and the Ellerbee Creek Railroad are also part of the outdoor fun.

Hundreds of butterflies soar in a spectacular world of wonder inside the Museum's three-story-high Magic Wings Butterfly House, with its lush foliage and tropical climate. Visitors explore the world of insects on a grand scale in the Aventis CropScience Insectarium. School groups learn science through hands-on programs in the second floor Lepidoptera Learning Lab.

For teachers, the Museum is an innovative science resource. In addition to workshops, overnight camp-ins, and year-round school programs, the Museum's professionals travel throughout the region to bring science to the classroom. Nearly half of the more than 100,000 students who experience the Museum each year do so through these outreach activities.

In 2005, the Museum will complete phase II of the Bio*Quest* campaign. This $14.1 million expansion will create the Down to Earth and Catch the Wind exhibits as well as a new Dinosaur Trail. Called a national model by the National Science Foundation, for zoos, museums, and botanical gardens, this

Bruce Feeley

The Museum aspires to cultivate discovery by providing engaging experiences. Here an educator teaches wildlife awareness with an animal program featuring the Museum's ferret. The Museum is home to many animal species, from the black bears of North Carolina to the Blue Morpho butterflies of Central America.

unique project is the first comprehensive plan that links animals and plants in their natural environment with interactive exhibits.

With a staff of seventy, the Museum relies on the support of volunteers, many of whom are members of the Youth Partners Program. Durham-area youth participating in this program receive real-world learning while working at the Museum and monitoring in middle schools.

The Museum of Life and Science is one of a select few in the world to be accredited by the Association of Science and Technology Centers. Ranked as the southeast region's fourth best museum destination by Family Fun magazine, the Museum draws nearly one-third of the population in the Triangle to its doors each year. These admissions, along with memberships, and foundation and corporate funding, support the Museum in its ongoing efforts to stimulate scientific experimentation and imagination and to encourage discovery and understanding of the natural world.

The Museum of Life and Science is a regional science and technology center on a seventy-acre campus in the heart of Durham. Two floors of hands-on exhibits, a nature park, a butterfly house, and a train ride allow for indoor and outdoor exploration. Visitors can also enjoy lunch or a snack at Caterpillar Café.

Bruce Feeley

Ask anyone where to go for the best hot dog in town and they'll point you directly to King's Sandwich Shop. For sixty years, King's has ruled from the corner of Geer and Foster Streets. Across from the Durham Athletic Park, King's has fed its share of hungry baseball fans. Today, King's is serving yet another generation of fans—those whose parents have been regulars of the tiny stand over the years. In addition to chili-smothered hamburgers and hot dogs smeared with mustard and laden with slaw, the King's menu still includes sausage or fatback-filled biscuits and icy cold drinks. Co-owner Bobby Sugg (seen here), chowing down on one of his creations.

Tim Wright

PSNC Energy

Reliable and affordable natural gas service has been the hallmark of PSNC Energy for almost sixty-five years. Now a wholly-owned subsidiary of SCANA Corporation, PSNC Energy serves more than 360,000 customers throughout north central and western areas of the state—some of the nation's most rapidly growing and economically successful markets.

As a proponent of economic development and quality of life in North Carolina, PSNC Energy integrates its corporate resources into the needs of the communities it serves. "We value the partnerships we have with local chambers of commerce and economic development organizations to attract and retain industries in North Carolina," says PSNC Energy President and Chief Operating Officer, Charles E. Zeigler, Jr. "In Durham County and in the Research Triangle Park we work hand in hand to make natural gas available for industrial expansion and relocation." PSNC Energy also demonstrates a strong commitment to enhancing the overall quality of life in Durham and throughout the state. From teaching children good study habits at Homework Centers to allowing employees paid time to mentor in schools, PSNC Energy is helping students. PSNC Energy also sponsors the Salvation Army's Heat Care Fund, which provides assistance to needy, disabled and elderly individuals who need help paying their heating bills.

"As partners in the growth and progress of our state, we are committed to making our communities better places in every way we can," says Zeigler.

PSNC employees work with children in Homework Centers in two of Durham's public schools. "We've enjoyed development of the Durham and Research Triangle Park area," says retired PSNC Energy President and COO Charles E. Ziegler.

Donna Jarnigan

The Vietnam Veterans Living Memorial honors Durham County veterans who gave their lives in service during the Vietnam conflict. But that monumental sacrifice was lost on the vandal who destroyed the granite monument in January 2001. Undeterred, community leaders Tim Holloway and Steve Laws joined creator and veteran Jerond Belton to rebuild the monument. By Memorial Day, the wounds began to heal as the temporary monument, seen here with Belton, was revealed.

This Vietnam Memorial will stand, not only as a symbol of immortality, but as a reminder of the bravery of those individuals who sacrificed their lives. This memorial will give us the opportunity to pause and reflect on the meaning of freedom as well as acknowledge the price we must pay to protect it.

GOD BLESS THIS GREAT NATION

We, the Vietnam veterans, honor and respect all the families and loved ones of those who served and fought for freedom in Southeast Asia.

We, the Vietnam veterans, salute all veterans who stand before this living memorial.

Chuck Young—Both

Blue Cross and Blue Shield of North Carolina

Blue Cross and Blue Shield of North Carolina (BCBSNC) is forging a healthy future for the state by using innovation to make its services more convenient and efficient while remaining ever-mindful of its heritage as a good neighbor to North Carolinians.

With over two million members, BCBSNC is the state's largest health insurer, offering a wide range of options for individuals, families and employers. The

The striking glass building of Blue Cross and Blue Shield of North Carolina is a landmark in the Triangle area. Completed in 1973, the rhomboid-shaped structure houses the headquarters of the state's oldest and largest insurance company.

company's diversity and quality products focused on member needs have repeatedly earned BCBSNC a Commendable Accreditation from the National Committee for Quality Assurance.

But that status was also achieved by an overall commitment to promoting healthy lifestyles and preventative health care. BCBSNC constantly develops new wellness programs such as the value-added Blue Extras,℠ including Alt Med Blue℠ (discounts on alternative medicine), Vita Blue℠ (discounts on vitamins and supplements), Optic Blue℠ (discounts on laser vision correction), and Blue Points℠ (incentives for physical activity). BCBSNC also provides members and other residents with information to help them lead healthier lives through *Active Blue,*℠ a

David Murray—Both

quarterly health and wellness magazine, and through the online Healthy Library, which offers health tips and related links. And by calling Health Line Blue,^{SM} a 24-hour health information line staffed by registered nurses, members can find answers to health concerns when and where they need them.

BCBSNC's web site is just one example of how the company puts innovative technology to work for members and providers. Online services allow employers and providers to handle administrative matters, provide brokers with online premium rate calculations, and give members ready access to service and information formerly available only by phone. In fact Blue Cross and Blue Shield of North Carolina was named one of *Information Week* magazine's top technology innovators for the year 2000.

Since it was formed in 1933, BCBSNC has served North Carolina communities and worked to keep them healthy. BCBSNC supports organizations, programs, and events that encourage and promote good health for children, encourage physical fitness and activity, and provide medical screenings and education for underserved areas.

President and CEO Bob Greczyn (center) with employees (l-r) Tarsha Carpenter and Edward Cho in the on-site Cyber Café. Since becoming CEO of BCBSNC in April 2000, Greczyn has rebuilt the company on the principle that high performing employees are the company's greatest asset.

Each year, BCBSNC employees volunteer more than 22,000 hours to help improve the health and well-being of their neighbors. They rebuild homes, tutor and mentor, host career opportunities, spend time with the elderly and homeless, walk for medical research, and support initiatives that build stronger, healthier communities. The management team also contributes through board service with local and national nonprofit organizations.

In 2000, BCBSNC launched a new, private foundation with $15 million to fund a variety of programs that promote health care access, education, and healthy lifestyles. This foundation is just one of the many innovative ways that BCBSNC will continue to be a champion for healthy living in North Carolina.

^{SM} *Service Marks of the Blue Cross and Blue Shield Association*

Over the years, the Duke Blue Devils football team has seen fifteen seasons without a loss at home. Since 1929, that home has been Wallace Wade Stadium (originally Duke Stadium), arguably one of the nation's finest collegiate football stadiums. With the netting of the 2001 national championship title (opposite), Duke's Blue Devils men's basketball team was honored by the president himself. For the third time, Coach Mike Krzyzewski (see inset) led his team to NCAA victory and then on to the White House. There, President George W. Bush, finding difficulty in pronouncing the coach's name, shortened it to simply "Coach K." Returning to Durham after the trip, the Blue Devils were met with great fanfare at rally on the Plaza.

David Murray—Both

132

DUKE BLUE D...
2001 NCAA CHAMPS

DURHAM, NORTH CAROLINA
The Herald-Sun
Established 1889
SOUVENIR EDITION

50 cents

DEVILIRIUM!

Ken Hawkins—Both

North Carolina Mutual Life Insurance Company

For over three decades, Mutual Plaza has risen high above the Durham landscape. But this home of North Carolina Mutual Life Insurance Company is far more than a city landmark. It is a symbol of more than a century of strength and perseverance, a monument to a people guided by the philosophy that self help leads to financial success.

Founded in 1898 as an answer to the insurance needs of the African American community, North Carolina Mutual has grown into one of the oldest and largest minority-managed life insurance companies in the world. Today North Carolina Mutual has offices in nearly a dozen states and is licensed to oper-

---

In the Heritage Room at North Carolina Mutual, visitors can get an in-depth look at the events that shaped the company into the largest African-American-owned insurance provider in the nation.

ate in nearly ten more. Its assets include more than $27 million in reserves and surplus and the company has nearly ten billion dollars of insurance in force.

A talented group of visionaries has led North Carolina Mutual through its long and challenging history. After surviving a claim in its first year of operation, the company reorganized in 1900 with two original founders, John Merrick and Dr. Aaron M. Moore, joined by local professional Charles C. Spaulding. Known as "The Triumvirate," this group led the company through a period of expansion beyond Durham and on to national prominence.

These early years were a period of trial and error, complicated by a lack of confidence from the financial community and the absence of trained personnel. In resolution to the issue of building a quality workforce, these early leaders began networking with local educators. This belief that self-improvement is essen-

Chuck Young–All

tial to success is still an fundamental element of the company's operations.

Today President and Chief Executive Officer Bert Collins is guiding the company through diversification of service and product offerings. While the company remains committed to its mainstay of providing home service products for families of modest income, the role of the agent in the field has become more productive with the advent of technology. North Carolina Mutual has also entered the corporate mainstream at the request of public and private entities who turned to the company for bids on group life insurance plans. Its clients now include many of the nation's Fortune 500 companies as well as local government and educational organizations.

Furthermore, North Carolina Mutual has found considerable success by marketing its universal life products in the workplace. In addition to endorsing this optional program, employers handle premiums through payroll deduction.

While these newer programs are now reaching a far greater market share and making North Carolina Mutual more profitable than ever, their greatest benefit is to consumers in the form of reduced costs and lowered risks.

Like his distinguished predecessors, Collins' business acumen complements his community leadership. He leads by example as a board member of various business and community organizations including a seat as past president of the Greater Durham Chamber of Commerce.

This sense of social responsibility and corporate philanthropy has been a thread of the North Carolina Mutual fabric since its inception. An early concept of the "Double-Duty Dollar," meant that the company's financial gain would be returned to the African-American community in the form of jobs, opportunities for homeownership and business start-up, and improved religious and educational facilities. Streets and schools throughout southeastern states still carry the names of North Carolina Mutual employees who have long been looked to as outstanding leaders and citizens as well as business professionals. Today, executives and employees still participate voluntarily in civic and social activities at the local, regional, and state levels.

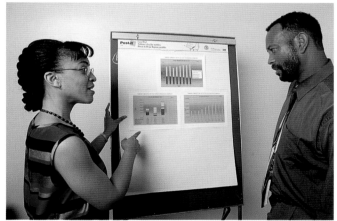

Top: Employees reach out into the community by participating in activities as volunteers of various agencies. Here, they mentor students at the Durham County Library. Above: Senior officers review premium income and growth progress on a company project. North Carolina Mutual's eye on trends over time has helped the company grow.

Above: By remaining committed to the company's mainstay clientele while developing new products, President and CEO Bert Collins maintains a balance between past successes and future growth. Collins also continues to foster the belief that community leadership is an important role of the company. **Below:** Historically, North Carolina Mutual's employees have been looked to for their leadership skills. Today, many still volunteer their time to make policy and raise funds as board members with area organizations such as the Boys and Girls Club.

Chuck Young–All

To honor outstanding individuals who have made significant advances for the benefit of African Americans, the company's board of directors established the prestigious Merrick-Moore-Spaulding National Achievement Award in 1967.

Addressing the needs of a more dispersed community has led North Carolina Mutual to focus on service as its primary offering today. While Internet pay plans are still on the horizon, newly integrated technology is opening doors for improved processing of collections and claims, development of new product lines, better management of existing offerings, and more productive sales results. But it is the goal of North Carolina Mutual Life Insurance Company to always offer the most appropriate products in the most efficient manner that will ensure the company and the community's future.

(l-r) Senior officers Chairman Nathan T. Garrett, President and CEO Bert Collins, and Executive Vice President Willie T. Closs, Jr., provide guidance for the board of directors and North Carolina Mutual by establishing the vision for the company.

One of the most magical times of year happens at Christmas when neighborhoods all across Durham display their lights in a fantasy arrangement of colors, designs, and exhibits. Driving through neighborhoods known for their array of outstanding light displays has become a tradition at Christmas as much as "trimming the tree."

Jim Wright—Both

When it opened in 1943, the Raleigh-Durham International (RDU) Airport saw only a handful of flights per day. Three years later, the number of daily flights rose to twenty-two. But it was the mid-1960s before the first Boeing 727 landed on the runway and three decades after that before the first international flights took off. Today, the number of passengers passing through RDU is growing to nearly one million per month. Since its opening in 1955, the terminal has undergone numerous expansions, the latest resulting in more than three dozen gates for arrivals and departures. From the Observation Park, airplane enthusiasts can picnic and listen to control tower communications while watching the activity on the ten thousand-foot runway.

David Murray

Measurement Incorporated

When your staff numbers regularly fluctuate by hundreds of employees, it helps to be flexible in your company's operations. But that's just one of the reasons Measurement Incorporated has grown to become one of the nation's largest educational testing companies.

At year's end 1979, Henry H. Scherich, Ph.D. left a job with another testing and research company and started Measurement Incorporated (MI) as a two-person operation out of his basement. The company quickly outgrew the basement as testing evolved from all multiple-choice exams to those which include some short answer questions and essays. MI began the practice of hiring temporary staff to handscore thousands of these assessments at various times during the year.

Today, MI employs a permanent staff of approximately 144 persons and more than twice as many temporary personnel at its Durham headquarters. Its Durham facilities include two adjacent historic buildings in downtown. Ten other scoring centers located throughout the eastern and midwestern states employ thirty-two full-time and several hundred temporary staff. MI's services have also expanded and now include test development, research, printing, data processing, and score reporting, and the company now handles assessments in mathematics, science, social studies, and foreign language in addition to English language arts.

Although managing large numbers of temporary employees presents challenges, MI has built a solid reputation for consistently high standards of quality. These standards are ensured through mentoring by permanent personnel and the continual employment of many long-term temporaries consisting of accomplished educators and business professionals who have undergone extensive training.

MI also upholds its dedication to quality by considering the human element of its operation. In addition to offering flexible work schedules and telecommuting positions, the company also allows parents to bring their children to the office on occasion when the need arises, and families are sometimes included in business

David Murray—Both

President Henry Scherich with A'Mari Gill, child of employee Kimberly Cozart-Gill. Rather than have work go undone, Scherich allows employees to bring children to work when they are out of school. A family-friendly atmosphere has contributed to Measurement Inc.'s success.

trips. These working conditions earned MI a Platinum Rule Award in the Family Friendly category from the *Triangle Business Journal* in 2000.

MI's staff are also given time out of the working day to participate in school-related activities, and many spend hours serving on the boards of non-profit organizations in the area. "What's important in the world is helping people and being part of a community," says Scherich. "And I think that a business that has good employees needs to encourage those employees to be a vital part of the community."

Furthermore, the company's resources are utilized to help improve writing scores in local schools as MI staff present teacher workshops and score local student writing samples. During the 1999-2000 school year, MI's workshops and volunteer tutoring at Y.E. Smith Elementary helped raise the number of fourth-

Measurement Inc.'s test development and handscoring quality is unparalleled in the industry. A solidly educated and experienced staff ensures tight quality control through a series of measures that include multiple reviews of outgoing materials.

grade students with passing writing scores from 9.1 to 39 percent. The company also hosts Youth Looking at the Future Today and National Groundhog Job Shadow Day, mentorship programs that help students apply their education to the workplace.

For its participation in local education endeavors, MI received the Durham Chamber of Commerce's 1997 Education: Top Priority award for mid-sized business. Today, the company's efforts continue to be rewarded through the knowledge that its support of education is ensuring a solid future.

Northgate Mall has an exciting new attraction for every member of the family. Here, Tracey Harris and her children, Parker and Annie, enjoy riding on a twenty-eight-foot Americana Carousel which is owned and operated by The Brass Ring Carousel Company, LLC, of Charlotte. With handcarved molds and handpainted designs, each horse on the ride took more than one hundred hours to produce. In addition, this distinctive carousel has a menagerie of animals including a dragon, reindeer, and zebra.

North Carolina Central University

When Dr. James E. Shepard chartered a private educational institution in 1909, he envisioned a place that would prepare African-Americans to be leaders in their communities. In 1923, that school became the nation's first publicly-funded liberal arts college for African-Americans. Today,

that educational facility is North Carolina Central University (NCCU), a catalyst for social and economic development among minorities and all racial and ethnic groups.

Since its founding, NCCU has forged a reputation for academic excellence in liberal arts studies. Its schools of law, business, education, library and information sciences, and its department of nursing, have produced leaders in their respective fields, many of whom hold national distinction.

But while its legacy remains firmly rooted in the liberal arts, NCCU is fast becoming a competitor in the scientific research arena. In 1993, the school's programs underwent a reformation in order to strengthen the science curricula. Today, NCCU's liberal arts programs are enhanced by a strong focus on the sciences at the undergraduate level.

This new emphasis on science has culminated in the development of the Julius L. Chambers-Biomedical/Biotechnology Research Institute (JLC-BBRI). Opened in 1998, the JLC-BBRI provides students with opportunities to participate in advanced research using sophisticated technology. A $12 million, 40,000 square foot, state-of-the-art facility, the JLC-BBRI is designed to be a research and training institute dedicated to those diseases that primarily affect minorities or African-Americans.

The first programs at the JLC-BBRI have focused on the study of cancer and its prevention, infectious agents that affect chronic diseases, the mechanisms of drugs of abuse, and the relationship between blood pressure regulation and cardiovascular disease. In the cardiovascular study alone, JLC-BBRI has already taken the lead in research by identifying a system that offers potential for the treatment of hypertension.

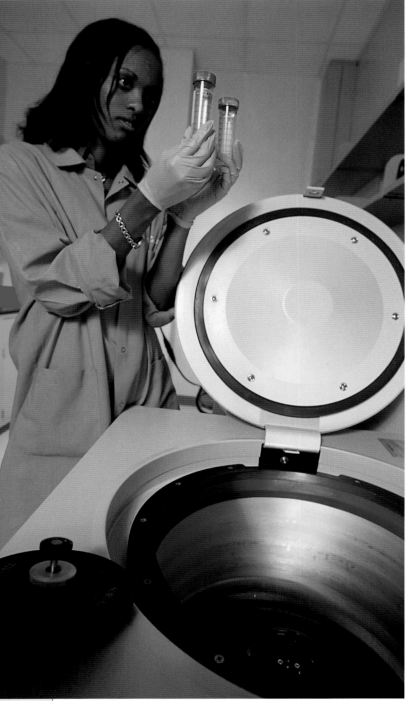

David Murray

In the JLC-BBRI Research lab, students like Ayne Adenew participate in research on various diseases, focusing primarily on those that affect the African-American community. Today, NCCU is placing special emphasis on the sciences and research.

NCCU also provides its graduates with a competitive edge by preparing them to communicate with people from all walks of life. Through its Academic Community Service Learning Program (ACSLP), NCCU requires its students to complete a total of 120 volunteer hours utilizing their unique talents for the benefit of worthy projects in the community.

Students in the ACSLP program can be found tutoring in schools, working in hospitals, cleaning neighborhoods of debris, promoting racial understanding among youth, and fostering a sense of pride among those the university calls neighbor. NCCU is one of only ten universities in the nation that teaches its graduates to be more civic-minded by requiring a specified number of community service hours for graduation.

Situated on a 130-acre campus, North Carolina Central University offers its students a wealth of academic resources as well as social, cultural, and recreational opportunities. It is an environment that fosters challenge and growth and prepares students to be the leaders of today and tomorrow.

(l-r) Students Lavoris Hutcherson, Jamar Pharr, and Michael Lawlar in front of NCCU's new state-of-the-art School of Education. Within its walls, students find the technology and instruction they need to be educators in the twenty-first century.

Bruce Feeley

Fishing is a favorite pastime for some in the Triangle region and the opportunities for a prize catch abound in the area's rivers and lakes. Jan Hackett of North Carolina Anglers and Outfitters especially enjoys fishing for bass in the Eno River. The largemouth variety, along with bluegill, catfish, and crappie, are some of the choice catches of the day in the region.

David Murray—Both

Chuck Young

When the Lipscombe family built their plantation in 1775, little did they know that two centuries later it would still be a place of respite. Today, as the Arrowhead Inn, this carefully restored estate offers a relaxing stay for weary travelers. Nine guest rooms include the secluded Carolina Log Cabin, complete with fireplace and lofted bedroom. The six-acre property owned by Phil and Gloria Teber includes a lush garden landscape that invites escape from the hurries of the day. And what better way to begin the day than with a breakfast of baked treats such as blueberry French toast or puffed pancakes. At right, two ladies pause to enjoy ice cream and a moment of conversation on the steps of Saint Joseph's Episcopal Church downtown, near Main and Ninth Streets.

Ken Hawkins

Mutual Community Savings Bank

At Mutual Community Savings Bank, business is about making a difference in peoples' lives.

Founded in 1921 by four minority businessmen with $425, Mutual Community built a reputation as a friend of low- to moderate-income people pursuing the dream of homeownership and financial security.

Today that humble building and loan association has grown into a $67 million publicly-held, minority-managed institution offering a variety of checking, savings, and loan products to customers. In addition to its main office and a branch in Durham, Mutual Community's Greensboro branch has extended opportunity throughout more of North Carolina.

Mutual Community provides all financial services through two locations in Durham and a branch in Greensboro. Customers are people here, not just numbers. And each is greeted by the friendly, familiar faces of long-time employees who work one-on-one with customers to ensure that each receive a quality service or product tailored to meet their needs.

As participating members of the community themselves, Mutual Community's personnel understand the needs of its clientele. The bank is also a community supporter, contributing to local public venues and participating over time in programs that develop affordable housing and educate the public about wealth management. These days Mutual Community is a primary lender for construction and renovation of area churches.

Through technology and a focus on personalized service, Mutual Community Savings Bank will continue to expand its offerings. But its top priority will always be personalized attention to the financial needs of the people it serves.

Chuck Young

Mutual Community Savings Bank's striking brick and glass headquarters symbolizes the strength and commitment of a bank with more than three-quarters of a century experience. While its appearance and product offerings are evolving, the bank remains steadfast in its philosophy of delivering personalized attention to its customers and the people of the community.

Ken Hawkin

David Murra

Each year, George's Garage and Cafe Parizade host the Spring Greek Extravaganza. Held at the Durham Armory, the spectacular event features a lavish buffet, bands, and a clarino player. The Aegean Dancing Troupe from Raleigh (top) performed in traditional dancing garb at the 2001 gathering. The Cafe Parizade also hosts a Greek Night, which closes out the summer and signifies fall is near. In its first decade of existence, the Manbites Dog Theater Company roamed from space to space, presenting its performances in rented rooms at various locations, typically former retail outlets. Today this alternative performance group is housed in its own theater on Foster Street, where it continues to bring unique—sometimes controversial—productions to the people of Durham. You never know what they'll do next at Manbites Dog. In 2001, the group left its theater for the great outdoors to present a Puzzlehunt, a performance-based scavenger hunt that drew eighty teams in search of the prize. Backstage a musician warms up for the production of "A New Fine Shame: The Life and Loves of Lou Andreas Salome" which tells the story of forward-thinking Victorian's influence on those around her including Freud and Nietzsche.

Every year, the campus of North Carolina Central University takes on a sweet, hopping vibe as the Grady Tate Jazz Festival comes to life. For two days in 2001, the sounds of jazz filled the B.N. Duke Auditorium as NCCU's Jazz Ensemble and its Faculty Jazz Group presented their own unique renditions of popular and all-time favorite pieces. Solo artists accompanied the groups, including a vocal performance by the famous jazzman himself, Grady Tate.

Ken Hawkins—All

The Forest at Duke

In an area dedicated to intellectual stimulation, advanced health care, and overall wellness, it just seems natural to find a life care community like The Forest at Duke. Here residents enjoy full independence and the support of services that carry them through the stages of life.

When The Forest opened in 1992, its founders—many of them Duke University faculty and alumni—made up a large portion of its resident population. Today, The Forest attracts retirees nationwide with backgrounds in health care, education, and a broad array of business professions. Residents Robbie and Trish Robertson enjoy the stimulating intellect of their neighbors. "We like the people," says Trish. "They're really nice people, interesting people. You can sit down to dinner with anybody and learn something."

Three hundred residences at The Forest range from a variety of apartment and cottage styles for independent living to 24-hour staffed assisted living suites and private nursing rooms. While this gated

David Murray—Both

community's lush, landscaped grounds and walking paths invite outdoor enjoyment, few residents will be found relaxing in the shade. "The backbone of this place is activity," says Earl C. Davis, in his eighties and still educating at Duke. "We're not sitting around rocking ourselves to sleep."

The Forest's Community Center is always alive with activity. In addition to housing both the formal dining room and casual café, this 40,000 square foot village center is the hub for educational, cultural, and social gatherings. Residents enjoy its auditorium and library, the arts studio, billiards room, full-service bank, gift shop, and hair salon. Down the hall are exercise rooms and an indoor swimming pool.

Frequent outings are part of daily life at The Forest. While local attractions are favorite day trips, nothing beats the excitement of college basketball. With three major universities nearby, residents have easy access to innumerable world class programs and activities.

Like other residents, Helen Corbett loves having so many things to do. But she was especially glad she had moved to The Forest before needing surgery. "When I came home I had to be in a wheelchair for six weeks and it was a breeze. They did everything,"

she says. "I was so thankful I wasn't in my house." In addition to the Health Care Center, which includes some days of prepaid care, The Forest's Wellness Center makes primary care accessible to residents.

Chris C. Hamlet typifies so many residents who "never say no" to volunteerism opportunities. In his nineties, Hamlet still delivers meals and remains involved with his church. Many Forest residents can be found volunteering countless hours in area hospitals, at local universities and museums, and for non-profit organizations, benefitting both children and adults. These substantial contributions are simply daily life for residents of The Forest at Duke—people who truly understand the meaning of community.

Above: The Forest honors special Durham residents by hosting the annual Council for Senior Citizens' "Over 90's Gala". Such events provide enjoyable ways for the Forest to give back to the larger community. Left: Outside the community center, residents spend a few moments catching up on Forest happenings. This "life oriented" community attracts retirees who want more than just an end to working, and offers a wide array of opportunities for continued service and personal growth.

U sing old-work techniques of forging, hammering, and shaping, Vega Metals creates contemporary works that are both functional and beautiful. This award-winning design team creates custom home furnishings and architectural pieces for both residential and commercial clients. But every project leaving this Hunt Street studio is more than shaped bronze or steel—they are works of wonder created by the hands of artists. Here, co-owner Neal Carlton shows one of the unique Vega Metals creations.

Chuck Young

Incorporated more than a half century ago, the Durham Art Guild is one of the oldest continuously operating visual arts organizations in the nation. Throughout the year, the Guild utilizes a Gallery (bottom) inside the Royall Centre for the Arts, which houses the Durham Arts Council. The Centre exhibits works in every medium from area artists. Each year, the Guild sponsors a non-juried membership show to encourage the display of any member's original work, as well as a Juried Art Show that draws artists of high caliber. The Guild works with area organizations throughout the year to promote interest in the arts which also focuses on the performing arts in the area. When Aaron Michael Moore III (left) returned to his native Durham, he brought home a family along with his artistic talent. That was the mid-1990s. Today, Moore has settled into his Amoore Art and Antiques studio and shop on Chapel Hill Street where he continues to

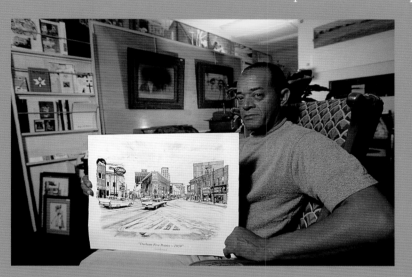

work on commission while recording his experiences over the years. Moore enjoys working in oils and other mediums, but he is perhaps most well-known for his pencil drawings. His "Durham—5 Points 1959" still hangs among several of his other works at the Durham Public Library. The drawing is one of his signature pieces that reveal downtown scenes of major cities in fine detail.

David Murray—Both

Central Carolina Bank

If ever a financial institution reflected the character of the community it serves, it is Central Carolina Bank and Trust Company. From its beginnings as a tobacco town to its moments in the spotlight as the City of Medicine and through to its future as a fertile ground for high tech companies, CCB has helped shape the city of Durham as well as the state of North Carolina.

CCB's sixteen story main office towers over the Durham landscape, serving as a beacon for those in need of solid financial products and services. Like its long-standing building, CCB will remain firmly rooted in the community that helped make it the banking stronghold it is today.

Celebrating its centennial in the year 2003, CCB has grown to more than 200 branches, but remains rooted in each community it serves. CCB's first customer was a young farmer who inquired about a $500 loan. The bank's founders, John Sprunt Hill and his son, George Watts Hill, devoted their lives to making that farmer's dreams come true, and to improving the quality of life for all Carolinians.

That tradition of service and leadership lives on in CCB's rapidly expanding presence throughout North and South Carolina. It lives on in CCB's involvement in promoting better primary and secondary education in the state. In health and social welfare. In the arts.

Chuck Young

David Murray

CCB sees education as one of its highest priorities. CCB recognizes outstanding educators through its Gold Star Teacher of the Year program in thirteen school districts. CCB associates serve on a number of education-related boards, including the Durham Public Education Network, the Durham Museum of Life and Science, and the Durham Workforce Partnership, a program designed to help ensure that graduating students have the skills to succeed in the workplace. CCB associates proudly lead the "Education: Top Priority" literacy tutoring program with the most volunteers by any corporation.

CCB also spearheaded the "Living in America" program, a practical financial education course for the Hispanic community.

Through charitable donations and volunteer efforts, CCB employees have established themselves as leaders in the support of the United Way.

CCB's growth rate in recent years has been phenomenal. The bank has been successful due to its ability to retain the touch and feel of a community bank while embracing the use of technology. CCB

CCB's charitable giving is well known throughout the state. American Red Cross representatives Pam Mears, chairperson, and Lynn Sherrill, chapter manager, receive a check from CCB's Steve Anderson to purchase a Disaster Services van. The van provides invaluable on-site disaster relief for North Carolinians.

has grown to anticipate and meet the needs of its customers.

CCB provides a complete line of personal, business, investment and trust banking services as well as full-service brokerage. CCB also offers a list of specialized services designed to assist business customers in collecting, managing, and investing their money.

Central Carolina Bank in the twenty-first century will be built on the heritage started by John Sprunt Hill by being a key resource in the communities it serves. CCB will continue to provide the broadest array of financial services for hardworking Carolinians who are building businesses, homes, and lives for their families and their communities.

Chuck Young—AII

At the Boy Scout Troop 400 Court of Honor, scouts receive their rank advancements and merit badges for work done since the previous court. In thanks for helping him make the first rank on the Trail of the Eagle, Omar McMillan places the parent pin on his father, Walton (above). Each month, Troop 400 participates in a major activity such as a hike or an overnight trip. There are more than sixty registered boys and fifty adult volunteers in this active troop. And since 1994, more than twenty members of Troop 400 have earned Eagle status. Cub Scout Pack 495 (far left) has been around for roughly forty years. Today its seventy-five registered members are guided by thirty-five adult volunteers. Both Troop 400 and Pack 495 are members of the Mawat District of the Occoneechee Council. Covering both Durham and Granville Counties, the Mawat District touts approximately 1,800 registered youth and nearly 700 registered adult volunteers.

DTW Architects & Planners, Ltd.

Throughout North Carolina, architectural structures created by DTW Architects & Planners, Ltd. represent more than solidly constructed foundations, they are physical testimonies to a relationship of trust forged between the firm and its clients.

With each of its projects, DTW Architects commits more than 130 years of experience to satisfying client demands regarding function, quality of material, and budget. But these professionals know that it takes more than experience to meet all the criteria of every project. That's why they pour creativity into each project, looking beyond the structure of a design to the needs of the people who will work and play in both the building and its surrounding environment. This insight, in part, is gained through involvement in professional and civic affairs at both the state and local levels including leadership in the American Institute of Architects of North Carolina (AIA NorthCarolina).

The open spatial design of the firm's studio contributes to its philosophy of being accessible and responsive to client needs. Clients are encouraged to be actively involved and can often be found here watching the process unfold. At least two of the firm's principal architects are involved in every project, promoting open communication that eliminates confusion and produces the desired end result. The firm also utilizes advanced computer technology to create three-dimensional visualizations and perform organizational tasks such as scheduling and tracking costs.

Founded by four native North Carolinians in 1978 as DePasquale Markham Thompson Wilson Architects & Planners, Ltd., the firm changed its name to DTW Architects & Planners, Ltd. in the early 1990s. Today the firm has grown to a staff of eleven, which includes four architects, technical specialists, and administrative personnel.

To date, DTW Architects projects include more than $700 million in educational facilities, office buildings, historical structures, public building, residences, and religious facilities. In addition to architectural design and planning for both new and existing structures, the firm's services have expanded to include total project management, facility studies, computer-aided design, and in-house model building. Beyond its own areas of expertise, the firm relies on its relationships with consultants in virtually all areas of building planning and construction.

With nearly 80 percent of its work performed on educational facilities, learning has long been a part of the firm's heritage. Students are invited to participate in the firm's activities and historical projects involve the efforts of the firm's archeological architects who work to educate the public about building significance.

But the firm learns from its clients as well, as exemplified by recent projects of design for high technology presentation lecture halls for the University of North Carolina. That ongoing desire to understand and satisfy client criteria will continue to bring DTW Architects & Planners repeat business and ensure its successful future.

Tim Wright—Both

Above: (l-r) Officers John Thompson, Robert Sotolongo, Frank DePasquale, and Lindsey Bute devote their combined talents to every project. First time clients are pleasantly surprised at the level of involvement in their projects by the principals of DTW. Right: (clockwise from lower left) Patricia, Robert, Fred, Lindsey, Dawn, Brian, Frank, Kim, John, Susan, and Paul comprise a portion of the DTW family. An open, welcoming atmosphere at the firm transmits beyond the walls to relatives and the community as a whole.

Bruce Feeley

There are more than sixty parks in Durham, and on Easter Sunday, hoards of youngsters gather at seven of them to join in the annual citywide Easter egg hunt. At the signal, as many as three hundred youth per park make one chaotic dash in search of the golden prize. Age groups ranging from three to twelve years are awarded a top prize, as well as three place prizes. For the older youth, the golden egg prize basket may contain a new basketball or remote-controlled car while the younger children receive stuffed toys and more. (l-r) Brandi Waters, Cameron Rustin, and Dashia Goodlow show off the coveted plastic eggs that contain sweet treats and maybe more.

Each Independence Day, families throughout North Carolina head over to the banks of the Eno River. That's when the place erupts in music, dance, and song during the Festival for the Eno. This three-day celebration is an annual fundraiser to help expand the Eno's parklands. Hundreds of artisans also attend the event, and no one can pass up the international food court. Over the many years, the festival has helped increase the size of Eno River State Park from its original few hundred acres to the more than 2,800 acres enjoyed by festival-goers today.

Bruce Feeley—Both

The Herald-Sun

While staying true to its long history of local ownership and a commitment to community journalism, *The Herald-Sun* in 2000 took major steps to expand its regional reach, to create special publications targeting niche markets and to further embrace electronic publishing.

"*The Herald-Sun's* mission is to be the community's essential and trusted source of news, information and commentary," said Publisher David Hughey. "Better than any other medium, we connect people in the western part of the Triangle with the local communities in which they live, while bringing readers and advertisers together. Our vision is to deepen our public service mission through the full integration of print and digital publishing."

The founding of *The Durham Morning Herald* in 1894 led to the creation of a closed-stock corporation called The Durham Herald Co. Since then *The Herald-Sun*, with a circulation of more than 58,000, has thrived on its mission to be the trusted and essential newspaper of record for Durham, Orange, and surrounding counties. In recent years, *The Herald-Sun* has combined a growing use of electronic publishing with a commitment to serve a wider regional audience and at the same time target niche groups in our community.

The result has been successful publications such as *Nuestro Pueblo*, a weekly page that delivers news and information in Spanish for a growing number of Latino readers, along with special sections for children and teenagers. *The Herald-Sun's* commitment to serving various groups in the community extends beyond the print product.

"*The Herald-Sun* and its employees are deeply involved in programs and activities that benefit the arts, education and families—areas we firmly believe are critical to the quality of life in our area," said Toby Barfield, vice president of sales and marketing.

Delivery alliances with such well-known names as *The Wall Street Journal* and *The New York Times* offer a vehicle for expanding the reach of *The Herald-Sun*, which is seen by 45 percent of adults in its primary market daily and 53 percent on Sunday. A new $3.8-million press has doubled color capabilities, and numerous other new systems—editorial pagination, library enhancements and financial systems among them—are helping *The Herald-Sun* offer continual improvements to readers and advertisers.

"We have made use of continuous improvement and Total Quality concepts to keep improving our product and better satisfy our customers, advertisers, readers and our community," said Vice President and Treasurer James G. Alexander.

In 2000, *The Herald-Sun* advanced its vision of the digital future by launching heraldsun.com, a comprehensive web site providing regional and national news and information with along extensive sections covering business, sports and entertainment.

Along with all the advances and new products, *The Herald-Sun* in 2000 continued its tradition of award-winning journalism, said Executive Editor William Hawkins.

"As the only locally owned newspaper and media company in our market, we enthusiastically pursue our mission of being the best source of news for and about our community," Hawkins said.

Left: *The Herald-Sun* **plant and printing press on Pickett Road in Durham is one of the most modern, state-of-the-art facilities in the state of North Carolina. Right: The new Goss Color Tower has doubled the color printing capacity of** *The Herald-Sun* **products.**

Sponsor provided—Both

The Durham Fire Department is pro-active in its approach to fighting fire. In addition to preventative programs for commercial properties, the department provides fire safety programs to the community in order to help citizens learn fire prevention basics. Beyond the firehouse, the department has also contributed to more than 5,700 activities in the community in the past few years. Fire personnel spend thousands of hours in training each month. At the Fire Academy, recruits and in-service personnel learn the proper procedures for extinguishing automobile fires. The Durham Fire Department's response time averages four minutes or under for a population of nearly 187,000 people in an area covering more than ninety square miles.

Chuck Young—All

David Murray

Everyone is a friend at the James Joyce Irish Pub. Located in the Brightleaf District, the James Joyce is a favorite gathering place for professionals and students alike. Dining here includes traditional Irish favorites such as beef and Guinness stew, fish and chips, and Gaelic chicken. And three nights a week, patrons are treated to live music. The James Joyce also offers a delicious catering menu for breakfast, lunch, or dinner.

Durham Regional Hospital

For more than twenty-five years, Durham Regional Hospital has been a good neighbor to the people of Durham and surrounding areas. It is a tradition of caring that began more than a century ago.

Durham Regional Hospital is the culmination of community efforts to provide quality, state-of-the-art health care. Newly constructed in 1976, it replaced two beloved facilities, the former Watts and Lincoln Hospitals. Founded around the turn of the century, these two segregated facilities gained favor in the community by employing caring personnel despite the lack of funding for modernization.

Today, Durham Regional Hospital, part of the Duke University Health System, is a 391-bed acute care community hospital employing more than 1,400 dedicated individuals. These professionals live by the hospital's mission to care for patients, nurture the sick, strengthen the well, and improve the overall health of the community.

Durham Regional Hospital provides comprehensive healthcare and includes a level 2 intensive care nursery, the Davis Ambulatory Surgery Center and Durham Rehabilitation Institute. The hospital also operates the Watts School of Nursing, which continues its legacy of producing recognized leaders in the field.

As a partner of the Duke University Health System, Durham Regional benefits from residency and research programs. These opportunities enhance a long-standing tradition of delivering quality, patient-centered care.

Durham Regional's campus provides the foundation for quality, compassionate care for the residents of Durham and its surrounding communities. By offering both patient-centered care for the sick, as well as outreach programs for the healthy, DRH is improving health for the community as a whole.

Les Todd

The Coquerel's sifaka is just one of the many wide-eyed wonders at the Duke University Primate Center (DUPC). Home of the world's largest captive collection of rare prosimian primates, the DUPC offers a chance to study and preserve animal species on the brink of extinction. While most of the curious animals living here are lemurs, the center also provides a welcome habitat for lorises, galagos, and tarsiers. Dr. Ken Glander pauses to visit with one of the center's prosimian primates.

Ken Hawkins

Don't panic—Durham hasn't been hit with a toxic spill (below). This is merely a classroom exercise at Durham Technical Community College (DTCC) as part of their highly regarded Environment, Health, and Safety Technology program. Operated by the city's public school system, DTCC originally opened in 1961 as Durham Industrial Education Center. Among the many programs offered then were practical nursing, drafting, and electronics technology. Today, DTCC continues to bring adults the education and skills they need to succeed in the working world. The college awards associate degrees in the arts and sciences, as well as degrees, diplomas, and certificates in areas ranging from business to public service. For many students in the Durham Public Schools, special partnerships with area businesses help prepare them for careers in the sciences, health care, business, finance, engineering technology, multimedia, law, government, or international studies. The Center for Health Sciences and Medical Professions at Southern High School (bottom) concentrates on the skills needed in the field of health care. As early as the ninth grade, students are introduced to clinical and hospital settings.

David Murray

Ken Hawkins

David Murray

Ken Hawkins

Ken Hawkins

The School of Law (top) at North Carolina Central University has been an integral part of the curriculum since 1940. By 1981, the school had moved to the Albert L. Turner Law Building, which serves to introduce students to the physical environment they will encounter upon graduation. In the moot courtroom law students come to understand procedures under the guidance of instructors and Dean Janice L. Mills (in front). The building also contains a state-of-the-art model law office, classrooms with computers, an extensive law library, and offices for student organizations. For nearly a century, North Carolina Central University has been a growing part of the Durham landscape. Today its more than one-hundred-acre campus is lushly landscaped to enhance its blend of modern and Georgian architectural structures. From the oldest building on campus, the Clyde R. Hoey Administration Building, to the new Julius L. Chambers Biomedical/Biotechnology Research Institute, students have access to every resource they need to fully develop as an individual. In the C. Ruth Edwards Music Building (above), students enjoy both studio and rehearsal space as well as classrooms for music, choir, jazz, and band courses.

Quality Communications, Inc.

In an area where some of the world's best-known telecommunication giants are making news, Quality Communications Incorporated (QCI) is making headlines in the lives of its employees.

QCI is changing the ways employer-employee relationships are normally viewed, by offering its employees opportunities for growth and development. With employees numbering over 400, QCI still keeps with the "small business" mentality of preparing employees for future success, by working hand-in-hand with employees and mentoring them for future achievements.

Bruce Feeley—Both

Based in Research Triangle Park, North Carolina, the company was founded almost fifteen years ago by its President, Robert E. Rigsbee, who iterates the importance of providing opportunity. "Because our management staff is open from top to bottom, employees truly believe in the opportunities of promotion the company presents to them. Due to the many people that have come through QCI at the entry level and worked themselves up to the management staff level, the opportunity itself stands alone as a sole motivator for diligent work ethics."

Mentoring of new employees by long-term staff develops into lifelong bonds that extend beyond the office into the personal lives of employees. Along with this mentoring, which helps employees develop socially, psychologically, and spiritually, QCI provides monthly evaluations and one-on-one training to step employees up the company's ladder of success.

QCI is a vibrant participant in community service

occurring at the grassroots level. The company sponsors senior-aged golfers in local tournaments as a means of paying tribute to the "pioneer golfers" that paved the way for the large numbers of minority participants that exist today.

QCI is also building a network and purchasing computers for a local church's after-school program. This collaborative effort is lessening the gap that exists in the number of computers between minority and Caucasian households while increasing opportunities for children's exposure to current day technology. QCI's donation of $250,000 is helping another local church build a self-sustaining school for inner city youth. In this isolated school on the outskirts of Durham, children will learn not only classroom studies but also life-sustaining skills such as farming and gardening.

Through high school and college internships, students are learning the technical aspects of jobs at QCI while gaining an understanding of the administrative responsibilities occurring behind the scenes.

For local clients like Duke University, North Carolina Central University, Time Warner Cable, and MCI WorldCom, QCI provides state-of-the-art telecommunications and information highway services, while its worldwide services extend to AT&T, Bell South, Verizon and IBM.

As future doors of opportunity open to the company, QCI will replicate these prospects for employees by providing avenues for growth and achievement. "Because employees see the high level of success established by management staff, they are able to set identical goals of high standard," says Rigsbee. Thus, demonstrating the company's motto "Get Quality First" as the overall criterion of QCI.

Far Left: President and CEO Robert E. Rigsbee knows that building a business is all about building people. Rigsbee fosters growth in the company and the community by openly providing opportunity for anyone attempting to succeed in life. Left: Through extensive training, QCI is able to maintain its high quality standards and retain nearly 80 percent of its workforce. One-on-one training for new employees helps them improve technical skills, progress successfully through the company, and be competitive with other applicants.

Bruce Feeley

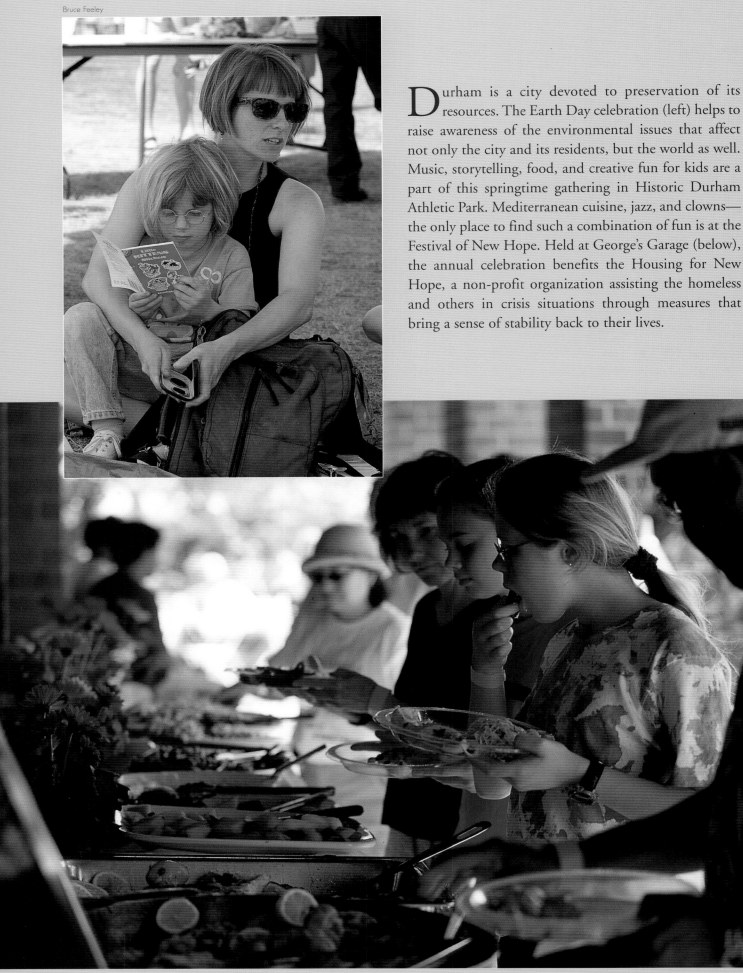

Durham is a city devoted to preservation of its resources. The Earth Day celebration (left) helps to raise awareness of the environmental issues that affect not only the city and its residents, but the world as well. Music, storytelling, food, and creative fun for kids are a part of this springtime gathering in Historic Durham Athletic Park. Mediterranean cuisine, jazz, and clowns—the only place to find such a combination of fun is at the Festival of New Hope. Held at George's Garage (below), the annual celebration benefits the Housing for New Hope, a non-profit organization assisting the homeless and others in crisis situations through measures that bring a sense of stability back to their lives.

Ken Hawkins

Chuck Young

Amid the excitement of the Bimbé Cultural Arts Festival, students of the Rites of Passage Youth Empowerment Foundation program showed off a little of what they had accomplished in a few short months. Led by founder Emily Gunter (shown here), the girls performed songs and recitations and presented their colorful depictions of the festival's many exciting activities. The program promotes personal and academic growth among the area's youth.

When the need to seek out and recover missing persons or evidence arises, the Sheriff's Search and Recovery Team is there. A unit of the Office of the Sheriff of Durham County, these professionals are certified Master Divers, able to operate in both zero visibility and hazardous conditions. As members of the Office of the Sheriff, the team is part of more than two hundred sworn officers and personnel, detention officers, and civilians who serve the county population of more than 223,000. Other units in the Special Services division of the office include the Emergency and Negotiation Response Teams and the Canine Unit. (l-r) James Utley IV, Barry Cayton, Donald Baker, and Roger Sipple.

David Murray

Featured Companies

AW North Carolina, Inc. *(page 81)*
4112 Old Oxford Highway
Treyburn Corporate Park
Durham, North Carolina 27712
Phone: (919) 479-6550   Fax: (919) 479-6580
By fostering an atmosphere of respect and appreciation, AW North Carolina has created a work environment of quality-minded people who produce automotive transmission components.

Blue Cross and Blue Shield of North Carolina *(pages 130, 131)*
5901 Chapel Hill Road
Durham, North Carolina 27707
Phone: (919) 489-7431
Website: www.bcbsnc.com
By combining innovation and a long tradition of caring, Blue Cross and Blue Shield of North Carolina is forging a healthy future for North Carolinians.

C.T. Wilson Construction Co., Inc. *(page 98)*
P.O. Box 2011
Durham, North Carolina 27702
Phone: (919) 383-2535   Fax: (919) 382-0044
Website: www.ctwilson.com
E-mail: chuck@ctwilson.com
By working through issues in advance and providing personalized service, C.T. Wilson Construction Co. has built a reputation as a leader in construction throughout the Durham area.

Cardinal State Bank *(page 89)*
3400 Westgate Drive
Durham, North Carolina 27707
Phone: (919) 403-2266   Fax: (919) 403-2166
Website: www.cardinalstatebank.com
Cardinal State Bank offers a full range of checking, savings, and loan options for individuals and commercial customers from branches in Durham and Chapel Hill.

Central Carolina Bank *(pages 156, 157)*
111 Corcoran Street
Durham, North Carolina 27702
Phone: (919) 683-7642   Fax: (919) 682-3870
Website: www.ccbonline.com
With a long heritage of building community, Central Carolina Bank and Trust Company provides a full array of financial services for Carolinians.

Cimarron Homes *(pages 116, 117)*
2330 Operations Drive
Durham, North Carolina 27705
Phone: (919) 382-2888   Fax: (919) 382-0414
Website: www.cimarronhomes.com
E-mail: scmcimarron@mindspring.com
Cimarron Homes has earned its reputation as the builder of beautiful and affordable houses that are helping Durham residents realize their dreams of home ownership.

Cormetech, Inc. *(pages 74–76)*
Environmental Technologies
Treyburn Corporate Park
5000 International Drive
Durham, North Carolina 27712
Phone: (919) 620-3000   Fax: (919) 620-3001
Website: www.cormetech.com
Cormetech, a leading company in selective catalytic reduction (SCR) of nitrogen oxides (NOx) from stationary sources, designs and manufactures SCR catalysts for a full range of electric power generation and process systems.

Croasdaile Farm *(pages 20, 21)*
2726 Croasdaile Drive, Suite 101
Durham, North Carolina 27705
Phone: (919) 383-5575   Fax: (919) 383-5577
Website: www.gardenviewrealty.com
Croasdaile Farm planned residential community offers residents of the fast-paced Triangle region the convenience of elegant living amid rural countryside, all within the city of Durham.

CrossComm, Inc. *(pages 84–86)*
One Peabody Place
112 South Duke Street
Durham, North Carolina 27701
Phone: (919) 667-9432   Fax: (919) 688-7686
Website: www.crosscomm.net
CrossComm's blend of artistic appeal with Internet technology produces visually stunning, yet functional web sites for non-profit organizations and businesses across the spectrum of industry.

DTW Architects & Planners, LTD. *(pages 160, 161)*
1121 West Main Street, Suite 201
Durham, North Carolina 27702
Phone: (919) 688-8102
Fax: (919) 688-8104
E-mail: dtwarch@aol.com
For DTW Architects & Planners, quality structures are about more than incorporating design elements and constructing with man-made materials—they're all about building relationships.

Duke University *(pages 62, 63)*
211 Allen Building
Durham, North Carolina 27708
Phone: (919) 681-3788
Website: www.duke.edu
As a major center of learning, Duke University is committed to excellence in academic education, medical research, athletics, and community service.

Duke University Health System
3100 Tower Boulevard, Suite 1300
Durham, North Carolina 27707
Phone: (919) 419-4623
Fax: (919) 401-9267
Website: www.mc.duke.edu

Duke University Medical Center *(page 79)*
1300 Erwin Road
Durham, North Carolina 27710
Phone: (919) 684-8111

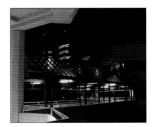

Compassionate patient care, education of professionals, and improved treatments through bio-medical research make Duke University Medical Center a leader in the field of medicine.

Durham Marriott at the Civic Center *(pages 14–17)*
201 Foster Street
Durham, North Carolina 27701
Phone: (919) 768-6000   Fax: (919) 768-6038
Website: www.marriotthotels.com
For business, pleasure, or meetings of any size, the Durham Marriott at the Civic Center is the premier place to stay in the city's center.

Durham Public Schools *(page 66)*
511 Cleveland Street
Durham, North Carolina 27702
Phone: (919) 560-2000   Fax: (919) 560-2007
Website: www.dpsnc.net
The Durham Public Schools offer a system that promotes both technological instruction while offering each student the highest potential for achievement. The schools are committed to ensuring each student achieves the highest education possible—whether it be Web site development, digital portfolios, database analysis, or instruction in general.

Durham Regional Hospital *(page 168)*
3643 North Roxboro Road
Durham, North Carolina 27704-2702
Phone: (919) 470-4000   Fax: (919) 470-8545
Website: www.drh.duhs.duke.edu
At Durham Regional Hospital, a century of caring combines with modern technology to provide patient-centered care in a community-based atmosphere.

Eisai Co., Inc. *(pages 92–95)*
900 Davis Drive
Research Triangle Park, North Carolina 27709
Phone: (919) 941-6920   Fax: (919) 941-6931
Website: www.eisai.com
"Human Health Care" is the philosophy that guides every employee at Eisai Inc. Located within the Research Triangle Park, Eisai is a state-of-the-art manufacturing facility, which also specializes in pharmaceutical and analytical research and development.

FOX 50 WRAZ-TV *(pages 102–104)*
512 South Mangum Street
Durham, North Carolina 27701
Phone: (919) 595-5050   Fax: (919) 595-5104
Website: www.fox50.com
Entertainment, sports, kid's stuff, news, and a sense of "doing the right thing" for the community make FOX 50 a favorite for family television viewing.

Greater Durham Chamber of Commerce *(pages 38, 39)*
300 West Morgan Street, Durham Centre, Suite 1400
Durham, North Carolina 27701
P.O. Box 3829
Durham, North Carolina 27702
Phone: (919) 682-2133   Fax: (919) 688-8351
Website: www.durhamchamber.org
E-mail: chamber@durhamchamber.org
Like this city of diversity, the Greater Durham Chamber of Commerce is multi-faceted with programs that focus on economic development, government affairs, business assistance, and community promotion.

Measurement Incorporated *(pages 140, 141)*
423 Morris Street
Durham, North Carolina 27701-2128
Phone: (919) 683-2413   Fax: (919) 683-1531
Website: www.measinc.com
Email: measinc@measinc.com
Measurement Incorporated provides state departments of education, private businesses, and a variety of educational agencies with testing development, scoring, research, and printing services.

M&F-Mechanics and Farmers Bank *(pages 107–109)*
2634 Chapel Hill Boulevard
Durham, North Carolina 27707-2800
Phone: (919) 683-1521
Fax: (919) 687-7821
Website: www.mfbonline.com
Providing quality service with a personal touch and addressing the needs of its communities continues to make M&F Bank a leader in the financial services industry.

Mutual Community Savings Bank, Inc., SSB *(page 149)*
315 East Chapel Hill Street
Durham, North Carolina 27702
Phone: (919) 688-1308   Fax: (919) 682-1380
E-Mail: mcsb@mindspring.com
At Mutual Community Savings Bank they look beyond the numbers to discover answers for the financial needs of the people they serve.

North Carolina Central University *(pages 144, 145)*
1801 Fayetteville Street
Durham, North Carolina 27707
Phone: 919-560-6295
Fax: 919-530-7976
Website: www.nccu.edu
For nearly a century, NCCU has prepared students to be leaders in their careers and in the community. Now it is leading the way in scientific research as well.

North Carolina Museum of Life and Science *(pages 124, 125)*
433 Murray Avenue
Durham, North Carolina 27704
Phone: (919) 220-5429
Fax: (919) 220-5575
Website: www.ncmls.org
The North Carolina Museum of Life and Science encourages scientific experimentation and understanding of the natural world through more than seventy acres of indoor and outdoor exhibits. "Where extraordinary science is an everyday thing."

North Carolina Mutual Life Insurance Company *(pages 134–137)*
Mutual Plaza, 411 West Chapel Hill Street
Durham, North Carolina 27701
Phone: (919) 682-9201; (800) 626-1899
Fax: (919) 683-1694
Website: www.ncmutuallife.com
From its roots as an insurer of African American families, North Carolina Mutual Life Insurance Company has grown into the largest minority-managed insurance company in the world.

Northgate Mall *(pages 70, 71)*
I-85 and Gregson Street
1058 West Club Boulevard
Durham, North Carolina 27701
Phone: (919) 286-4400   Fax: (919) 286-3948
Website: www.ngatemall.com
With Belk, Hecht's, Sears, and Old Navy anchor stores, more than one hundred specialty
shops, a scrumptious food court, a variety of services, and events throughout the year, it's no
wonder so many choose to shop Northgate Mall—where you find *everything under the sun!*

PSNC Energy *(page 128)*
P.O. Box 2008
Durham, North Carolina 27702-2008
Phone: (877) 776-2427
Website: www.psncenergy.com
As a supplier of natural gas and a responsible corporate citizen, PSNC Energy fuels homes,
businesses, and economic growth in Durham and the Triangle area.

Quality Communications, Inc. *(pages 172, 173)*
1812 Riddle Road
Durham, North Carolina 27713
Phone: 919-598-6585   Fax: 919-598-8203
Website: www.qcommunications.com
For over twenty-five years, Quality Communications has provided technology, support, and
resource solutions for some of the world's most demanding companies.

RTI *(pages 46–49)*

P.O. Box 12194	3040 Cornwallis Road
Research Triangle Park, NC 27709-2194	Research Triangle Park, NC 27709

Phone: (919)541-7044   Fax: (919)541-8737
Website: www.rti.org
RTI is an independent, non-profit research organization dedicated to conducting research that
improves the human condition. With a staff of more than 1,900 people, RTI turns knowledge
into practice in the fields of health and medicine, environmental protection, technology commercialization, decision support systems, and education and training.

Stubbs, Cole, Breedlove, Prentis & Biggs, P.L.L.C. *(pages 120–122)*
122 East Parrish Street
Durham, North Carolina 27701
Phone: (919) 682-9331   Fax: (919) 682-5590
A law firm that has deep roots dating back to 1932, with special emphasis in the areas of real
estate and banking but including representation in all civil areas and some limited criminal areas.

Syngenta Biotechnology, Inc. *(pages 24–26)*
3054 Cornwallis Road
Research Triangle Park, North Carolina 27709
Phone: (919) 541-5801   Fax: (919) 541-8585
Website: www.syngentabiotech.com
Syngenta Biotechnology, Inc., is a center of excellence in biotechnology research for Syngenta,
a world-leading agribusiness. Based in Basel, Switzerland, Syngenta has more than 20,000
employees in fifty countries who help farmers grow better crops through improved seeds and
crop protection solutions. Syngenta Biotechnology employs approximately 300 staff dedicated
to using biotechnology in crop genetics research and crop protection discovery for global food
chain solutions.

The Forest at Duke *(pages 152, 153)*
2701 Pickett Road
Durham, North Carolina 27705-5610
Phone: (919) 490-8000   Fax: (919) 490-0887
Website: www.forestduke.com
E-mail: marketing@forestduke.com
It is easy to be independent and active at The Forest at Duke, where residents enjoy comfortable accommodations, enriching amenities, and a full continuum of care.

The Herald-Sun *(pages 164, 165)*
2828 Pickett Road
Durham, NC 27702
Phone: (919) 419-6500   Fax: (919) 419-6892
Website: www.heraldsun.com
The triangle region's only locally owned newspaper and media company, bringing award winning journalistic news to Durham County, Orange County, and the surrounding area.

The Housing Authority of the City of Durham *(pages 52, 53)*
330 East Main Street
P.O. Box 1726
Durham, North Carolina 27702
Phone: (919) 683-1551   Fax: (919) 683-1237
Website: www.durhamhousing.org
The Housing Authority of the City of Durham is changing the face of Durham through initiatives that bring a wealth of services to residents and form the foundation for a successful future.

The North Carolina School of Science and Mathematics *(pages 30, 31)*
1219 Broad Street, P.O. Box 2418
Durham, North Carolina 27715
Phone: (919) 286-3366   Fax: (919) 286-7249
Website: www.ncssm.edu
At The North Carolina School of Science and Mathematics, high school students who show both an interest and a talent for science and mathematics excel in an atmosphere that promotes both learning and lifelong friendships.

Triangle Orthopaedic Associates, P.A. *(pages 56–58)*
120 William Penn Plaza
Durham, North Carolina 27704
Phone: (919) 220-5255
Fax: (919) 281-0371
Website: www.triangleortho.com
Triangle Orthopaedic Associates focuses on patient-centered care in its delivery of a full range of orthopaedic and pain management programs and services.

Verizon *(page 35)*
4100 Roxboro Road
Durham, North Carolina 27704-2122
Phone: (919) 317-5000
Fax: (919) 317-5631
Website: www.verizon.com
Verizon's comprehensive telecommunications solutions cover everything an individual, business, or government entity could need including outstanding customer service.

Washington Duke Inn & Golf Club *(pages 112, 113)*
3001 Cameron Boulevard
Durham, North Carolina 27706
Phone: (919) 490-0999, (800) 443-3853   Fax: (919) 688-0105
Website: www.washingtondukeinn.com
E-mail: reserve1@duke.edu
In the distinctive tradition of excellence instilled by the Duke family, elegant surroundings, exquisite cuisine, warm comfort, and gracious hospitality await guests of the Washington Duke Inn & Golf Club.

WTVD ABC 11 Eyewitness News *(pages 42, 43)*
411 Liberty Street
Durham, North Carolina 27701
Phone: (919) 683-1111   Fax: (919) 628-7225
Website: www.abc11tv.com
WTVD and the ABC 11 Eyewitness News team deliver news, information, and helping hands to the people of the Heart of Carolina.

Riverbend Books Team

Regina Roths, *senior writer.* Andover, Kansas. Roths has written extensively about business since launching her journalism career in the early 1990s. She is a graduate of Wichita State University. Her prose can be found in corporate coffee table books nationally, as well as area magazines, newspapers, and publications. Her love of history and extensive research on various subject matters give her a keen sense of vision for writing.

Bruce Feeley, *photographer.* Durham, North Carolina. Feeley has worked for twenty years throughout the northeast and North Carolina for numerous news organizations and editorial clients. He has been the principal photographer for The American Dance Festival since 1994. His work from the festival is represented in the Library of Congress, Local Legacies collection. A member of the National Press Photographers Association, his work can be seen in *The New York Times, Sports Illustrated, USA Today* and various travel publications.

Ken Hawkins, *photographer.* Marietta, Georgia. Hawkins has pho-tographed for *Newsweek, Time, Paris Match, Forbes* and *Georgia Trend*. He has photographed many international political events and figures. He is a member of the Paris-based SYMGA Photo Agency and A.S.M.P. Hawkins has received several photography awards, and was named Georgia Photographer of the Year.

David Murray, *photographer.* Kennebunkport, Maine. David was on the staff at the Ft. Lauderdale *Sun/Sentinel* for nine years before he started freelancing in 1989. His awards include the 1981 Pulitzer Prize finalist team in Spot News, runner-up for the Robert F. Kennedy Journalism award, and in 1986 won the NPPA/University of Missouri first place award in spot news.

Tim Wright, *photographer.* Richmond, Virginia. In his twenty years as a photographer, Wright's assignments have taken him from the Arctic to South Africa and across America. His publishing credits include *Business Week, US News & World Report, Smithsonian, Time, Air & Space*, and *The New York Times*.

He has a knack for telling a story with each photo.

Chuck Young, *photo editor and photographer.* Atlanta, Georgia. Young has a degree in photography from the Rochester Institute of Technology in New York, and has more than twenty years experience in photographing such clients as Coca-Cola, NationsBank, BellSouth, and IBM. He is currently the photo editor and senior photographer for the Bookhouse Group, Inc., of which Riverbend Books is an imprint.

Jill Dible, *designer.* Woodstock, Georgia. Jill is an accomplished book designer. She has eighteen years experience as a graphic designer, including eight years as art director for Longstreet Press. She studied Fine Arts at Bowling Green State University. Jill has designed books for such clients as the Arthritis Foundation, the American Cancer Society, the Federal Reserve Bank of Atlanta, Riverbend Books, and the Bookhouse Group.